Lawmen of the Old West

The Good Guys

Del Cain

REPUBLIC OF TEXAS PRESS

Dallas • Lanham • Boulder • New York • Toronto • Oxford

Republic of Texas Press is an imprint of Wordware Publishing, Inc.
No part of this book may be reproduced in any form or by
any means without permission in writing from
Wordware Publishing, Inc.

Printed in the United States of America

ISBN 1-55622-677-2
10 9 8 7 6 5 4 3 2 1
9908

All inquiries for volume purchases of this book should be addressed to
Wordware Publishing, Inc., at 2320 Los Rios Boulevard, Plano, Texas 75074.
Telephone inquiries may be made by calling:

(972) 423-0090

Contents

Acknowledgements

If I thanked everyone who deserved it, this section would be as long as the book. Without the guidance and example of my parents, Elmer D. and Frances Cain, I would not have had the interest in history that led to this. Without the patience and support of my family, especially my wife, Isabel, I would not have had the time or confidence to start it. Without the sharing and abilities of the "Good Guys" of the DFW Writers' Workshop I would not have the skills to write it. Without the kindness and insight of my editor, Ginnie Bivona, I would not have had the courage to complete it. Thanks to you all.

Preface

The dime novel myth of the good guy lawman in the Old West got a severe battering at the hands of real history. The most famous of the so-called heroes of the West turned out to be gamblers, politicians, and sometimes even outlaws. They were not the fighting men committed to upholding the law that we wanted to believe in. We were always a little uneasy with the ballads and stories that tried to make misunderstood heroes out of Jesse James, Sam Bass, and Billy the Kid but may have been surprised to find out that lawmen like the brothers Earp and Masterson and Pat Garrett were not a lot better than the men they were set to control. We think of Wyatt Earp as a lawman, but he served as one for at most seven years, and even while he held law enforcement offices, he was part owner of saloons or worked as a dealer in gambling halls. Bass Reeves wore the badge of a United States Marshal with honor for thirty-two of the toughest years for law enforcement in the Indian Territory. Bat Masterson spent very little time as an officer but became famous while Jeff Milton spent most of fifty years carrying a badge of one sort or another and is almost unknown. Perhaps our greatest loss came when we found that the escutcheon of the famed Texas Rangers was not entirely without blot. Like all men, they had flaws; many were great law officers and some were not. There were certainly periods during which some of them went beyond their mandate and furnished the punishment they thought malefactors deserved even when there were courts available that should have had that responsibility. Of course there were Rangers who deserve to be counted among the good guys. That those whose careers were spent primarily in the Ranger Service are not included here is in recognition that they have been written about more than any other body of law enforcement officers. It does not reflect on the record of their work.

The men depicted here were not perfect, either. They were hard men doing a difficult job in dangerous times. Their careers were not without controversy either in their time or ours. Several of them were tried for one crime or another but found, "not guilty." Then, as now, officers were often called upon to defend their use of deadly force in the courts. All of these men have had their detractors and still do. The lawmen included here all have records and reputations that I believe justify their inclusion in the group. If I had to pick a bunch from that period of history to side me in a fight, I don't think I could do any better for skill at arms, devotion to duty, or personal integrity.

We do not have to go without heroes. We do not have to choose between Wyatt Earp and Roy Rogers, knowing that neither of them is quite the real thing. We just need to look for the "good guys" and not expect perfection.

So, here they come; alike in many ways, committed to making communities safe by the application of the law. Men who learned the trick of not giving in to fear and had the skills with men and guns to accomplish the jobs that were set before them. It is not possible to make generalizations about why these men became the "good guys." They are not alike in other significant ways. Jefferson Davis Milton was the son of a Southern governor while Bass Reeves was an ex-slave. There were men born on the frontier like John Slaughter and Elfego Baca, on Midwest farms like Dave Cook, and Europeans like the Danish born soldier and

U.S. Marshal Chris Madsen and the fistfighting Irishman Tom Smith. Grant Johnson was a Creek freedman, with both African and Native American ancestors. Sam Sixkiller's ancestry included both Cherokee and European lines although he was an enrolled citizen of the Cherokee Nation. Many fought in the Civil War—some for the Union, some the Confederacy. Madsen fought in the Danish army, the French Foreign Legion, and the U.S. 5th Cavalry before becoming a law officer.

Tall men, short men, rich or poor, they were, without exception, fighting men. They were tougher than those who opposed them or we wouldn't be talking about them and—

Early law enforcement officers of Indian Territory.
(photo courtesy of the University of Oklahoma Libraries)

something we often forget—they were successful. Their efforts changed the places they served. Some found the excitement or satisfaction of what they did such an attraction that when they had brought peace to one town they moved on to another where their skills were needed. Others saw what they did as part of living in their community and only served as long as the need existed.

We want—we need—heroes. It is not hard to find them in the ranks of the lawmen of the Old West if we look beyond the flash and myth left by the writers of the dime novels. We can, if we look, find the "good guys."

Elfego Baca
The Indestructible

McCarty was under arrest. He was just pursuing a Texas cowboy's usual recreational activity of getting drunk and shooting up the town, in this case, Frisco, now Reserve, New Mexico. True, he had taken particular delight in shooting at a few citizens' feet to see them dance, but it was the drover's idea of fun. His friends were shocked. The very idea! Arresting a Texas cowboy for having a good time. When they came to free their companion they were well armed and fueled by large measures of righteous indignation, racial prejudice, and red-eye liquor. Unfortunately, McCarty's captor, Elfego Baca, did not want to give him up.

"I'm going to count to three and if you're still here, I'll assume you want a fight and start shooting."

They were so astonished to be challenged by a lone man and a "Mexican" to boot that they didn't move. Baca counted without hesitation or delay, and as he said "three," he opened fire. He apparently was not trying to kill anyone since it would have been easy enough at that range, but one of the riders took a bullet in the leg and the trail boss's horse reared and fell over backwards. The trail boss was fatally crushed. The drovers carried off the body of their leader and nothing more happened the rest of that day or during the night.

The next morning was a different story. Cowboys had ridden in from surrounding ranches and trail herds to help put down a "Mexican uprising." The "uprising" consisted of Elfego Baca guarding his prisoner. He was making plans to move McCarty to Socorro since a local justice of the peace did not seem inclined to stir up trouble for himself by angering the cowpunchers any more than they already were. After some early morning visits to Milligan's Saloon, talk became heated but was swayed by peacemakers who arranged for an Anglo justice of the peace to hear the case. Turning his man over to legal authority suited Baca, and the case was heard. McCarty was fined five dollars for disturbing the peace.

It was after the trial, when everyone should have been satisfied with the outcome, that things got rowdy. As Baca left the building there was some shouting and a shot was fired. Elfego knew he could not count on help from the residents of Frisco. He ran down the alley to a jacal, a small house made of branches set upright in the ground and plastered with mud. Quickly warning away the woman and children who were there, he settled in to defend himself. He had no time to get bored. Very shortly, a group of cowboys advanced on the house led by a man named Jim Herne. Herne had his gun in hand and announced that he had come to drag that "dirty little Mexican" out of there. He was carried away dying with two bullet holes in him.

That was just the beginning. The cowboys, perhaps as many as eighty of them, poured round after round into the flimsy little building. Fortunately for Baca, the floor of the house was dug out about a foot and a half below the level of the ground so he was able to stay low while his opponent's bullets tore through the walls. Whenever the shooting died down Elfego raised up enough to pick a target and seldom missed. The accuracy of his return fire was so effective that the attackers tied ropes between the adjacent buildings and hung blankets over them so that they could move around without being picked off. They spent some of their ammunition on a plaster statue of a saint on which Baca set his hat.

Near sundown, the bullets had weakened part of the jacal to the point that it caved in on him, and it took him a considerable time to dig his way out of the rubble. Without better light though, no one rushed him. Who wanted to face someone in a protected position who never seemed to waste a bullet? In the middle of the night, they came up with some dynamite. They threw it at the little house and destroyed about half of the building. They waited for first light to see if they had succeeded in killing their man. As the sun rose so did the smoke from what was left of the old chimney. Elfego was cooking breakfast. He had found some beef and other supplies, made some tortillas, and had himself a good meal.

Clever attempts to get in close to the house pretty much ended when a man using a cast-iron stove front for a shield managed to expose just a bit of the top of his head. Elfego promptly put a crease in it. The man was not badly hurt, but it discouraged anyone from trying something like that again. By that time Elfego had killed two more of the cowboys and wounded an unknown number.

After a day and a half of siege there may have been as many as four thousand shots fired. One version of the story claims that there were three hundred and sixty-seven bullet holes in the door alone and that a broom handle had been hit eight times. During the afternoon of the second day, Baca was hailed by J. H. Cook, who had negotiated the original agreement that got McCarty to court. Francisquito Naranjo, who had been the only citizen of Frisco willing to help Elfego arrest McCarty in the first place, accompanied him and a deputy sheriff named Ross from Socorro, a man Baca knew. They offered a deal. He would come out and surrender to Ross, and his safety would be guaranteed. After some wrangling he agreed—on the condition that they get everyone out in the open where he could see them and that he kept his guns.

It was a strange escort for a prisoner. Six of the cowboys were allowed to ride along, but they rode well ahead of the buckboard carrying Baca. They were to stay in plain view at all times. The wagon was driven by Deputy Sheriff Ross and behind him sat the "prisoner" with a pistol in each hand. They rode like that all the way to Socorro where Baca turned in his guns and allowed himself to be locked up in the town's new jail. Ironically, the partially completed jailhouse was being built on the old baseball field where Elfego had been born nineteen years earlier, interrupting the baseball game his mother was playing at the time.

After a few months he was transported to Albuquerque and tried and acquitted, not once, but twice, an occurrence that became something of a legend of its own in legal circles in New Mexico. During the trial, one of the more superstitious cowboys involved in the fight testified to his belief that Baca had some kind of magic charm that protected his life. He was sure that bullets would do no damage even if fired point blank at him.

At this point in his life, Elfego Baca was just nineteen years old and was armed with no more authority than moral indignation and a mail-order badge. This was the sort of combination that would have gotten an ordinary man killed. Not him.

He had gone from his home in Socorro, New Mexico, to Frisco near the Arizona border at the request of an acquaintance, Pedro Sarracino. Sarracino was a storekeeper and part-time deputy sheriff who had talked to Elfego in Socorro and complained that his town was so out of control he was afraid to try to arrest anyone. He told Baca about all the things that were happening that the law could not or would not undertake to eliminate. That was all it took to move Elfego to pin on his shiny new badge, pick up his guns, and head to Frisco to put things to right. There is little doubt that Baca went into this fight, as he did most things, with at least some thought to the future he planned in politics. Even so, along with politics as a constant theme in his life went a consuming passion for protecting the underdog.

Elfego Baca was the remarkable son of remarkable parents. Shortly after his birth on the baseball field at Socorro, the family moved to Topeka, Kansas, for increased opportunity and better education for the children. Since the range land in the area of Socorro was being increasingly taken over by Texas ranchers, who brought their wranglers with them from the Lone Star State, it is also possible that Elfego's mother, Juanita, wanted to get her husband away from the area before he got into too much trouble. The Texans had little tolerance for their Mexican-American neighbors, and Francisco Baca had little patience for insult. They lived in Kansas for fourteen years until Juanita's death.

That country was getting much too settled to suit the rest of the family so Francisco, the father, Elfego, and his brother Abdenago returned to the Socorro area in 1880. Francisco took the job of town marshal in Belen and soon revealed his lack of concern with his place in society by allowing a horse of his to win a race away from one of the leading lights of Los Lunas, a town some distance north of Belen. On top of that, when the man accosted him over the race results, Francisco whipped him soundly in a fistfight. Not long after that incident, he insisted that a couple of cowhands from the same town refrain from shooting up Belen. When the cowhands expressed a preference for continuing what they were doing and made the mistake of trying to also shoot up Francisco, he found it necessary to kill them. This was not taken very well in Los Lunas. It wasn't long before arrangements were made to grab Francisco and drag him off for a trial where the citizens could be reasonably sure of a conviction. He was quickly sentenced to spend a long term in the Los Lunas jail.

Elfego, then seventeen and a true son of his father, recruited a friend named Chavez and paid a visit to Los Lunas, arriving during the night while many of the citizens were recovering from the effects of celebrating a saint's feast day. They climbed into the second story courtroom directly over the cell holding his father and cut a hole in the floor. They pulled Francisco and two other prisoners up through the hole, and they all escaped through the window. They hid out in the tall grass directly across the road from the courthouse all of the next day. They were made comfortable by the supplies that Elfego had thought to bring along. The following night they watched the posse that had been searching for them return to town and give themselves up to rest. When all was quiet, they made their way out of town.

The Bacas and Chavez returned to Socorro, but Francisco went on to his brother's home near El Paso. Getting out of New Mexico and into Texas would avoid any repercussions arising from his having escaped from jail. Elfego stayed in Socorro. He knew what he wanted to do with his life. He wanted to enforce the law as his father had. He wanted, he said later, for the outlaws to "hear my steps a block away from me." Two years later he took on the cowboys in Frisco and became a legend.

Baca's reputation was solidified not long after his acquittal in Albuquerque. He returned to Socorro and found work. His cousin, Conrado, who was a partner in a general store and saloon in Kelly, a small mining town about fifteen miles away, came to him. Business was good, he said, but the miners and hard cases had discovered that the two partners would not defend themselves, and now most of their profit was being taken up by theft or used for target practice by the customers. They had come to Elfego to see if he would help. In fact, their plan was for Elfego to go to Kelly, straighten things out, and come back and let them know when it was done. It was agreed and off he went.

In Kelly, he found the store and saloon doing a great business even though no one was there to collect the money. In fact, that made the experience even better for the customers, and they seemed bent on drying up the saloon's liquor supply as fast as possible. When Baca challenged them to explain just what they were doing, several men made movements as if to draw their weapons. Instantly they were staring down the barrels of the pair of pistols carried by their challenger. The fact that they were so completely beaten to the draw caused a question to be asked. They wanted to know just "who the hell" this young man was who seemed so intent on spoiling their fun.

"I am Elfego Baca."

Suddenly there were good explanations for all that was going on. The men were just watching the store for the owners until they came back, but if Baca wanted, they would be glad to turn it over to him. Could they, please, just have one more round of drinks? That arranged, Elfego was in charge of the store. It was time to go inform his cousin that things were under control.

It didn't sit too well that the partners had not been willing to come with him and help take back their own. He thought about that overnight and the next day sent word out all around Kelly. He spent the day giving away merchandise, free, to everyone. It was a happy town.

When he got back to Socorro and explained what he had done, he asked if they had any complaints about the procedure. The two apparently swallowed hard and discovered that they didn't have any complaints, at least none they were willing to voice to Conrado's cousin.

Over the next few years the young man's reputation increased as he worked at different jobs, often more than one at a time. Some of the work involved wearing a badge, a real one this time. Among other things, he was a deputy sheriff and deputy United States marshal. He gathered the scars that went along with that type of work but was never down for long. It was Elfego who finally put an end to the career of a man named Jose Garcia who, after many other crimes, had killed a man in Belen and kidnapped his wife. He kept her for a while, but when he got tired of her he killed her, cut her body into quarters, and hung the pieces in a tree to dry.

There was an outcry from the people to bring him in, and after several other officers had failed, Baca went after him. He arrested him in a hideout in the hills and brought him in to the nearest town in order to catch a train. When he got there, he found another problem. The citizens were eager to apply their own brand of hempen justice. He had to hold off a mob until the next train arrived.

Sometime around 1890 Elfego started on the next step of his career; he began to study law with a judge in Socorro. Four years later he was admitted to the bar and quickly became as flamboyant and as effective in court as he had been as a law officer. He also continued his general disregard for procedure when he perceived it as interfering with the interests of justice. As a result there were few in the New Mexico courts, lawyers or judges, whose feelings about him were neutral. They either liked the color and concern he brought to his work or they hated the disruption and lack of tact of which he could be capable. It was not unusual for him to find great fault with a judge's personal characteristics and legal abilities when a ruling went against him. It was also not unusual for the judge to find that those assistants he depended on to help maintain order were not available for some reason when he became angry enough to demand Elfego's removal from the court. They didn't want to be the one to try to force Baca to do anything he didn't want to do.

For the most part, after the explosion, Baca would tell a story or joke and quickly put the judge back into better spirits so that the case could continue. That he held the respect of some is proven by the fact that soon after he began to practice, he joined forces with Judge Freeman, who had recently spent a term on the state Supreme Court. Freeman was well known and well respected, and Elfego began to exercise his legal muscle as a partner in the firm of Freeman and Baca.

As always, it was not enough for Baca to be involved in only one thing. From the base of his practice, Elfego ran for a variety of offices in the county and city and served in capacities ranging from mayor to county superintendent of schools to district attorney. He never had any difficulty getting elected.

Public office and a law practice did not take up the energies of this ever-busy man. Along with numerous business interests, he found time to get involved in politics in Mexico. His contacts started with a trip he made before the revolution.

Baca had gone to Mexico to bring back a cross-border cattle rustler. His interest stemmed from the rather sizable bounty that was offered for the man's capture. He found his man, Doreteo Arango, nicknamed Pancho, but notice came that the offered reward had been cancelled. This fact along with a growing regard the two men shared caused Elfego to forget about the errand he had started. In later years, he told of their attempt to develop a mine together and of their trips by Model T to the mine site in the mornings, tossing beer bottles along the roadside. On the trip back, they amused themselves by shooting the empty bottles as they drove past. Neither of them missed very often.

A few years later, they were not on such good terms. Baca was named personal representative in the United States by General Huerta during the short time he held power in the struggle of the generals to control their country. Elfego's old friend Pancho, now using the surname Villa, was not happy that his former partner was associated with his mortal enemy. Villa made some serious threats. Relations were not improved by a scheme of Baca's that resulted in something of a revolt against Villa. That plot allowed Baca to obtain one of the four custom-built Mauser rifles that the revolutionary leader had ordered from Germany. Pancho offered a reward of $30,000, American, for anyone who would return his rifle and kill his old friend. Elfego was disappointed a little later when United States Army troops under John J. (Black Jack) Pershing began the hunt for Villa and ruined a new plan he had worked out which he expected would bring the reward money to him and see Villa dead.

It was not a total loss, however, since when Baca was later in Washington he had instructions to present himself at a certain bank to claim the fee he had earned for his assistance to General Huerta and his defense of Huerta's ally General

Salazar. He had made great efforts to get Salazar freed when the general was arrested and charged with violating the neutral status of the United States by fleeing across the border after losing a battle in the competition of the generals for control of the new government of Mexico.

When Elfego presented his claim, he was asked to name his fee. The only figure that came to mind was the reward that Villa had put on his head. He set the price at thirty thousand dollars. It wasn't until later that he discovered he was operating in a different climate than he was used to. He could have asked several times that much, and no one would have blinked.

In the meantime, Salazar was still in custody in New Mexico. After much bother, he was finally transferred to the Bernalillo County jail in Albuquerque where his attorney, Counselor Baca, could have access to him. Soon after the move, the general was on his way back to Mexico following a well-organized jailbreak. There were some suspicions raised when it was noticed that at just the time of the unplanned release, Elfego Baca was in a local bar conspicuously asking various reputable citizens for the time so that he could set his watch. He had been quite vocal all during the affair about his belief that the United States had no legal right to hold a military officer of a neighboring country without charge or hearing. Did he act on that conviction? There were no charges filed.

There was a later incident that some thought might have been related. During a trip to El Paso, a man named Celestino Otero asked Baca to meet him at a small café to discuss a "private" matter. When Elfego arrived in a car driven by a friend and saw Otero approaching the car, he got out and went to meet him. As he came around the vehicle Otero pulled a gun and fired a shot, causing a slight wound to Baca's groin. Being in his fifties and carrying a comfortable paunch did not have much effect on Baca's old skills. Before Otero could fire again, Elfego drew and fired twice. Two bullets went directly through the heart. Once again, the man who came to kill Baca was dead. The rumors that the shooting had something to do with the freeing of General Salazar from the jail in Albuquerque ran rampant, but when the trial was over the jury took only long enough to canvas themselves. The verdict was "Not Guilty."

In 1919 Baca realized one of his earliest ambitions; he ran for sheriff in Socorro County. He won, of course. Then he did something so typically "Baca" that some people could not believe that it worked. He gathered all the outstanding warrants that the office was responsible for serving and wrote letters to the wanted parties. He informed them that he had a warrant for their arrest and ordered them to report to his office to surrender. If they did not come in, he would come after them in the belief that they intended to show fight and would shoot them when he found them. Some reports say that most of the recipients of those letters turned themselves in. It is certain that some did and probable that others decided that Arizona, Texas, or some other location had a climate more suited to their health. In either case, it took little time to clear the new sheriff's warrant list.

While sheriff, Elfego had the kind of close call that really could have hurt the reputation of the "indestructible." Two young accused outlaws were in his jail awaiting trial. One of them had been made a trusty and put to work in the kitchen. One day he saw his chance and slipped out the door to freedom. The sheriff hated to spend the time needed to go after him, and besides, it might become necessary to kill the young man if he resisted. Elfego didn't want that for someone who had never been convicted of anything. After much thought, Baca finally released the escapee's partner, took him out to eat, and gave him a deputy's badge, a gun, some handcuffs, and some money. He ordered him to go find his friend and bring him back and promised that, if he did that, the judge would know about it and it would be considered at his trial.

After several days, and a good deal of ribbing from his friends, Baca started worrying. It began to look as if he would have to go after the both of them and would never live the incident down. He might even have to resign. After a long week, he was saved from that embarrassment but irritated all over again. It cost him $8.75 in collect charges to get a long telegram, which detailed every step the cowboy had made in catching up with his partner and what he had gone through to get those handcuffs on the man. It ended with a question. Now what was he supposed to do? Elfego's response used all ten of the words that the minimum telegram charge provided: "Kiss him twice and bring him in you damned fool."

In the meantime, Baca ran the sheriff's office just as he had lived all of his life. He made his own decisions and did what he thought was right. When the state legislature passed a law allowing debtors to be incarcerated until they could pay their debts, the Socorro County jail was soon full. It made no sense to Elfego. How were these people supposed to take care of their debts from a jail cell? He simply turned them loose with the advice that they had better find work and pay what they owed. Any objections to that plan were met with the explanation that it cost the county too much to feed them. The district attorney was not happy, but before a major confrontation could arise, the law was repealed.

As he neared sixty, a time when many men would be entering or at least planning for retirement, Baca continued to fill

13

Elfego Baca
(photo courtesy University of Oklahoma Libraries)

his life with the kind of excitement only very special characters ever generate. He continued to practice law and was called on occasionally by acquaintances in high places for assistance. When Albert Fall became President Warren G. Harding's secretary of the interior, he grew tired of continual complaints from ranchers in southern Utah about Paiutes running off livestock and being very uncooperative about returning them. Fall arranged a deputy United States marshal's commission for Elfego Baca, who only needed it for a short time. The problem was solved.

Never shy about talking, especially about himself, Elfego was invited to speak at a meeting of the New Mexican Cattle Growers' Association meeting. They held that one in Magdalena, in the section of the state where he had been born and made his name. He spoke and, as always, kept his audience entertained. At the dance following the meeting, trouble started. First, there was a young cowboy who prodded the "old man," trying to provoke a fight with the apparent intention of creating an instant reputation for himself. When the boy started to draw his pistol, Elfego proved that his hands had not lost their touch, but he didn't bother with his gun. A fist in the face was enough to take the fight out of that one.

This led an older Texan named Saunders to get involved. Saunders had something of a name already, although it is possible that he had fabricated his own. He claimed to have killed three men in gunfights. When he tried his luck on Baca, he hadn't cleared leather when Elfego's gun was out and pressing into his body. Then the "old man" took away his weapon and gave him a quick start for the door with a boot in the backside.

Later, in his hotel room, word was brought to Baca that Saunders had re-armed himself and was busy in a saloon with some friends, talking threats and taking on a load of liquor courage. Elfego Baca had never waited for trouble to come to him. He put on his guns and headed for the bar. He faced Saunders and his friends down with his eyes and stepped to the end of the bar. He carefully removed a pistol from its holster and laid it in front of him as he ordered a round for the house. His eyes moved from man to man, making sure that everyone took the offered drink.

As they drank, nervously it may be assumed, Elfego talked to them. He joined in the language that they had been using. He, too, was a "wild Texas cowboy" and hated those "damned Mexicans," and he liked to drink with others like himself so they all better have another round. When that was down, he turned his attention to the bartender. He was still casually fiddling with the gun on the bar. Surely, he suggested, those drinks were on the house for such a fine bunch of Texas cowboys as they were, weren't they? That suddenly sounded like a fine idea to the bartender so Elfego picked up his gun and marched out. The is no record of any further trouble with the man named Saunders.

For a time, he was the chief of security (he referred to his job as "chief bouncer") at the Tivoli, a grand casino in Juarez. He oversaw the work of fourteen security officers who undertook to protect the peace and safety of the customers and to guard the place from the robberies that were common in all the establishments of that nature in Juarez. After hearing what the leader of the gang responsible for the attacks had to say about him, Baca hunted the man up and made a suggestion that the criminal leave both Elfego Baca and the Tivoli alone. The suggestion was accompanied by some physical punctuation that was designed to make clear the point that he was still a man to be reckoned with. Apparently, the lesson took; there were still raids on gambling houses in Juarez, but never on the Tivoli while he was in charge.

Some years later, Baca decided to move his law practice to Albuquerque, and, knowing he would need time to get established, arranged for an appointment to a county position to help support himself. He had not been in town long when he saw an Albuquerque police officer arresting someone he knew. He was not happy with the treatment being given the man being arrested and expressed his displeasure with a big silver pocket watch that he carried in his vest pocket on a chain. This application was good for neither the policeman's head nor the watch. Baca was taken before the judge at the city night court. No one knew him there, and the judge offered him a choice. He could pay ten dollars and court costs or serve thirty days in jail. He took the jail time.

When the court constable got him to the jail, he turned him over to a startled guard and left. Elfego, who had just recently taken over his duties as chief jailer, then recorded himself as a prisoner, released himself on his own recognizance, and filled out the paperwork which would allow him to collect the jailer's fee for Elfego Baca, prisoner, for the next thirty days. The fee was just about right to replace the broken watch.

He never changed, and the stories go on and on. In his later years in Albuquerque there was a man who claimed that Baca owed him three hundred dollars. The dispute raged back and forth for months. One day the creditor caught Elfego on the street and told him that he wanted to ask a question.

"If someone owed you money and wouldn't pay, what would you do?"

"I'd sue the son-of-a-bitch!"

Sure enough, a few days later Baca was served with papers announcing that a suit had been filed for the recovery of the three hundred dollars. He responded instantly and typically.

He sat down at his desk and made out an invoice. "For legal advice requested and acted on—$300." With his usual directness he hand delivered the bill, and the debt was cancelled.

He was a colorful character and one whose career was filled with controversy. Nevertheless, it should never be forgotten that he made himself the law officer that he wanted to be. Politics aside, when he was wearing a badge and his guns, the "bad guys" definitely "heard his steps a block away."

Dave Cook
Officer and Organizer

Dave Cook was mad. The summer of 1859 was gone, winter would not be far off, and someone had stolen their poke. Dave, who had just turned nineteen, and his younger brother, sixteen years old, had dug long and worked hard to accumulate the small bag of gold they had kept hidden away in their cabin. It was enough to keep them going through the winter. They had not had the luck of some in the Colorado gold fields, but they were making a living. The younger brother despaired. They would never be able to dig enough out of their claim before the weather shut them down. Dave's response was "keep digging."

While his brother worked the mine, Dave checked his gun, saddled his horse, and started talking to people around the little mining settlement of Missouri Flat, Colorado. Most of the people he talked to were sure that no one local would steal gold from a miner. After all, in lieu of any organized law enforcement, the rule was simple. If someone was caught stealing, he was hung. There was no more to it than that. There were no officers, no jail, no courts, and certainly no appeal. Dave was unconvinced. None of his friends, who couldn't believe someone they knew would do such a thing, could remember any strangers around the settlement. He was

sure that if someone new had been around long enough to figure out who to rob and how to pull it off, he would have been
noticed. It had to be someone they all knew.

Eventually, he had checked all the camps and mines in the
area and could account for everyone who should be there. The
men who worked the mines, the teamsters, and those who
cared for what little commerce such a small mining camp
offered were all where they were supposed to be. In his mind
he listed the men he knew by category, and when he was
about to give up, it occurred to him that he had not seen Jerry
Tolman, a sort of ne'er-do-well who had been hanging around
the camp for several weeks. Tolman was, to use a phrase of
the time, work brittle and had never been seen to do much of
anything. A quick check of the community showed Dave that
Tolman was gone and no one had seen him since the robbery.
While they continued to express their doubts about Tolman's
guilt and Dave's ability to find him, they let him know that if
he did find the man and he had the gold, they would help
hang him. They did not want to see someone get away with
that kind of theft in a mining camp.

Dave "went on the scout" looking for a lead to where
Tolman had gone. He began an outward spiral from Missouri
Flat, keeping his eyes open and talking to everyone he came
across. He found two miners working an outlying claim who
had seen a man "like that" headed east. With the trail found,
Dave was on it. After two days, he had followed the track to
Golden, a few miles from Denver. His man had been seen
drinking in a saloon and buying supplies, but no one knew
where he had gone. Once again, Dave circled. He moved out
from town a little farther each time and finally found a trace
to follow. About noon of the second day out of Golden, Dave
got his break. Tolman was evidently sure he was well away
and safely set up in the brush and canyon country. He let

down his guard. He made a fire to cook his noon meal. The smoke brought a visitor he did not expect.

Caught cold and covered before he could defend himself, Tolman threw himself on the mercy of "the court," in this case, Dave Cook. He turned over the gold and begged Dave not to take him back to Missouri Flat to be hung. Dave had seen a man hung earlier by a so-called "people's court" in Denver. He was not in sympathy with the bad guys, but he was uncomfortable with that sort of execution of justice. With his gold back and feeling the decision was his to make, he turned Jerry Tolman loose and pointed him east. It would be a rare exception. He was to become known for bringing in the one he went after and doing it according to the law.

The Cook brothers spent two years working their claim and saving their gold. Apparently, Dave had no other thoughts as to what he would do with the rest of his life but to buy a farm back in Kansas and work it as his father had done. As the Civil War was starting, they sold their claims, packed their gold, and headed home. Dave intended to enlist in the Union army as soon as he got there.

The war was just beginning, and confidence was high. No one seemed to believe it could take more than a few months at most to settle things. That being the case, Dave bought his land and started farming. It did not look like the Union really needed his help.

By the summer of 1861, things had changed. The war was not going well for the North, and the fighting was getting close; battles had been fought in Missouri, and the divisions of opinion in Kansas were increasingly bitter. Dave was restless and hurried to finish getting in his crops so he could enlist. When he tried, he got a surprise. The Army didn't want him for a soldier. They looked at his experiences in Colorado, particularly a time when he had worked as a freighter, and sent him to Rolla, Missouri, to run supply trains as a civilian employee.

The trains were rich finds for troops in gray, western guerillas, bandits, and hostile plains Indians. He found his hands full protecting the supplies and getting them through to the troops who needed them. It didn't take long to discover that more supplies disappeared than could be accounted for by raids. The Indians were always blamed but could not have stolen as much as they were being given credit for. Dave had to know where the supplies were going. A little quiet investigation showed that the main thieves were men working on the supply crews, often cooperating with soldiers in the Army supply system. When he was sure who the culprits on his train were, he nabbed them. They were turned over to the Army authorities suffering from some bruises and black eyes. Stealing ended on the supply trains captained by Dave Cook.

When the Army understood what had happened, Dave was taken off supply train duty and assigned to put an end to pilfering from all the supply system of the Army in the West. It took him a month to figure out and expose a corrupt operation that was being run by a group of enlisted men and civilians in the Quartermaster Corps. That accomplished, he tried to enlist again, but his reputation would not allow it. Once again the Army decided they had use for his special talents. He was sent to the ordinance department of the Army of the Frontier to find and stop more thievery. Like the first time, his success was quick and complete. The result of this triumph was to get him sent back to Denver. He was going back to where his career got its start. He was assigned as first assistant to Alden Warwick, the chief government detective, and given the task of stopping losses from the forts making up the Colorado military district.

"Well, maybe somebody ought to just ask them."

Warwick was stunned by the response. He suspected that the young man just assigned as his assistant was taking the problem too lightly. He had just explained the extent of the losses and the fact that none of the stolen goods ever reappeared. The amount of supplies and number of horses stolen from both the forts and from the local civilians indicated a large number of thieves. The lack of success the officials had had in tracking them and the complete disappearance of the stolen goods and animals made the detective believe they were up against a well-organized criminal effort, and this new assistant, hardly more than a boy, was pulling his leg about it.

"Wasn't joking. They must hang around here somewhere. Somebody who kept his eyes and ears open might learn something. Might try it myself." Warwick looked shocked; "They're killers. Anybody who tried that wouldn't last long."

Cook shrugged, "Isn't that part of the job? We have to stop them, besides might as well make our part of the war exciting. I've tried to enlist twice, but the Army won't give me a uniform. They want me to chase thieves. I'd rather chase Rebels."

In spite of that feeling, Dave agreed with his new boss that if they could put a stop to the theft of supplies meant for the troops on the front lines, they would be making a larger contribution to the effort than they could as individuals in that line. It was agreed Dave would work with no apparent connection to the government, arrange his own housing, and handle the investigation his own way. He knew Denver, and he knew the kind of men he was up against.

He found a room in a cheap boardinghouse in a section of town made up mostly of saloons, gambling houses, and businesses of even less repute than those. He began making the rounds of gathering places, giving the impression of a young man looking for a good time and a way to make a living that did not involve too awful much actual labor. He watched and listened and became an easy part of the life of the rougher side of Denver. After a few days, his interest centered on a couple of men who seemed to rate a considerable level of respect among the rougher crowd. They were known only by the nicknames Google-eye Ed and Smiley. Believing that they were the caliber of men who could run the kind of operation he was determined to stop, Cook began to spend his time hanging around the saloon they favored. They were there every night, and Dave was there to keep an eye on them.

A night came when they did not show up. Dave hunted for them in all the saloons and other places of amusement in Denver. He had no luck. The next morning he got a surreptitious message from Warwick. During the night the homes of three citizens had been burglarized and ten horses had been stolen from the government corral. The thefts had been carried out quietly, efficiently, and there were neither clues to who did it nor traces to show where the property had been taken.

The next evening Cook began to get closer to his prey. He invited Google-eye and Smiley to sit in a card game with him and dropped the hint that he needed to find a way to make some money without too much effort. He told them he had been keeping his eyes open and had come to the conclusion that they were smarter than most of the others around there and probably could steer him the right direction.

It came out in bits and pieces, but within a few days the two had let drop most of the secrets of the gang's methods, had admitted they were the leaders, and were begging their new friend to join them. The setup was efficient but involved many more people than the authorities had guessed. There were a dozen hard cases who handled stickups and burglaries and about twice that many handymen, laborers, and others who fed them information on the wealthier homes. Through them the crooks always knew who had valuables, where they were kept, and how they were protected. They had the best of information on when houses were left unwatched for a week, a day, or an evening.

The situation with thefts from the Army was a little different. A number of enlisted men from the fort took horses or supplies and sold them to a saloonkeeper at the edge of Denver, who then delivered them to Google-eye and Smiley. Left unknown was what they did to get rid of the loot.

Dave had a plan to take care of that detail. He arranged through his boss to have a trustworthy soldier make a deal with the "fence" to sell an Army horse. Cook, with another agent, W. Frank Smith, to back him up, hid out to keep watch on the saloon. The soldier tied the horse out front, went in, and in minutes came out and walked away. Almost before the trooper was out of sight, the saloonkeeper's assistant came out, mounted the horse, and headed for tall timber. Cook and his partner followed the man for fifteen steady hours of travel away from Denver. Finally, almost a hundred miles from their starting place, the rider met two others he seemed to know. While they were talking, the two detectives struck. With the men in custody they searched the little hollow and found ten other Army horses and several more stolen from civilians.

The capture was made immeasurably more useful by the panic of the two horse guards who, in hopes of mitigating future punishment, babbled out everything they knew. Dave ended up with lists of gang members, hiding places, and other evidence that would help convict the thieves. Now all they had to do was catch them.

They returned to Denver using back trails and slipped into the fort after dark. Warwick arranged for three squads of cavalrymen, one each led by himself, Dave Cook, and Smith. They hit the two main gathering places of the gang members and their storage warehouse at the same time. With neither warning nor suspicion, the gang gave up without a fight. There were more stolen horses found to add to the twenty-two brought back by Cook and Smith plus thousands of dollars' worth of stolen goods and Army supplies. Ed and Smiley went to jail threatening all sorts of terrible revenge on Dave Cook, their downfall.

Under military law the criminals were convicted and sentenced to long terms in federal prisons. They could not be executed for their offences as they would have been if tried in the "people's courts" of the day. The two outlaw leaders arranged to correct that problem sometime later. They broke out of prison, but before they could carry out their threats, vigilance committees, cheated out of their earlier opportunity to show how they felt about the thieves, lynched them both. Stamping out that gang did not end larceny or violence in Denver, but it eliminated the only real organization of the time and left it easier to concentrate on controlling the rest.

Dave was a federal employee, and, as such, his responsibility was to the Army. However, since Denver was under martial law at the time, he was often called upon to help solve crimes against civilians. His reputation was made when he crushed the "Ed" and "Smiley" gang and continued to grow as he spent long hours in the saddle and resolved case after case. Those long rides, sometimes a hundred miles or more, to chase down an outlaw whose crime had been committed in Denver planted the seed of a new idea. Law enforcement in the western states and territories was a haphazard mess. Official officers were responsible for solving crimes that occurred in their county or municipality and arresting the criminal no matter how far away he escaped. They had to deal with a jungle of conflicting and overlapping jurisdictions and often could expect little help from other officers, who were overloaded with their own work or, in some cases, more sympathetic with the outlaws than with their pursuers. Because of this, much crime went unsolved. Even worse, when the perpetrators were generally known, they often escaped justice by the simple expedient of hiding out in a jurisdiction where they knew the law would ignore them or help them.

The end result of this disjointed law enforcement effort was citizen unrest that led to the formation of "vigilance" committees. These groups of citizens, generally fueled by outrage, took hold of the reins of justice and resolved matters to their own satisfaction. This sense of rightness usually led to a branch on the nearest tree or to a crossbar nailed on a telegraph pole. The problem, to Dave Cook's way of thinking, was that summary justice often ignored rules of law and occasionally ended up hanging the wrong man.

Determined to find a better way, Cook recruited a group of men in Denver and the surrounding towns to act as sort of a permanent vigilance committee. He carefully chose men who could not only handle themselves when the going was tough but who had reputations for reliability and integrity. They were sworn to secrecy and tightly organized to pass on information about crimes and criminals and to join in the chase whenever it involved their territory. The biggest difference between this group, which Dave called the Rocky Mountain Detective Association, and earlier vigilance committees was that they were committed to turn all prisoners and evidence over to the proper authorities. There would be no lynching. Cook's strongest hope was that the Rocky Mountain Detective Association would turn out to be so efficient that the law enforcement officers of the territory would want to partici-pate, and dependence on civilians could eventually be decreased. Within a few weeks the organization was set with twenty-five men in Denver and fifty in the surrounding towns and countryside. They were ready for their first test, and they didn't have to wait long.

Some horses were stolen in Denver, and the alarm went out. Dave took to the trail hoping the organization would be able to prove itself. It worked even better than he had expected. He tracked the thieves toward Golden, and just as he arrived in town the agents of the Association brought in the stolen horses and the thieves. Within a few months so many outlaws had been captured before they could get away with their loot that crime in the entire Denver area had dropped so low it seemed like a new place. In fact, things were so quiet that Cook made a third and final attempt to get into the war.

In early December 1863, without a word to anyone, he quietly enlisted in the First Colorado Cavalry. It didn't work. His enlistment was allowed to stand, but he was immediately put on detached duty and assigned to the office of govern-ment detective in Denver for the duration of the conflict and "except in cases of fighting emergency." He was disappointed, but the feeling didn't last long. The reason for that decision became clear a few weeks later. Alden Warwick was trans-ferred, and Dave Cook, just twenty-three years old, was made Chief Government Detective for the Denver area. One advan-tage of his promotion was to give him the opportunity to define "emergency" as it regarded his service to the military. While he didn't "get into the war," as he really wanted, he did see action several times in fights with plains Indians. They seemed prepared to take advantage of the white invader's pre-occupation with fighting among themselves and began raids aimed at discouraging further settlement.

His only war-related action came when he rode out as part of a cavalry unit dispatched to meet a band of guerillas who had come up from Texas to invade Colorado and hold it for the Confederacy. The guerillas, however, had irritated some citizens by raiding local ranches and "liberating" supplies. By the time the Army arrived, there were only eight of the invasion force left alive to take into custody.

When the war ended, so did Dave Cook's job. He didn't see any immediate prospects for something to do so he began to make plans to return to Kansas and the farm he had purchased almost four years earlier. Those plans did not get very far before his friends and supporters convinced him he was needed in Denver, and they nominated him for city marshal. He was elected in April of 1866 by a wide margin. Among his first actions was to appoint his friend from federal service, W. Frank Smith, to be his chief deputy and to notify the Rocky Mountain Detective Association that they would remain in business.

As marshal, Dave acted as he had during his entire career; he relied on planning and organization to reach his goals but was always ready when the case called for action. Kitty Wells, a dance hall girl in the least reputable part of Denver, was savagely beaten by her lover, Sanford S. C. Duggan. He had been living with Kitty and existing mostly on her income for a couple of years. During a quarrel he beat her over the head with his pistol. This was the type of crime that went largely ignored by most law officers in the West. As long as the residents of the shady side of town confined their criminal activities to each other, they were generally left alone. This was not the way Dave Cook saw the law.

Dave went looking for Duggan and found him in a saloon. Duggan punctuated his description of what he would do to

Cook by waving around a drawn pistol. Dave drew and fired, wounding the young tough, disarmed him, and hauled him off to jail. This incident enhanced Cook's already good reputation, but more than that, it served notice in the tougher quarters of town. What they did would no longer be ignored just because they were careful where they did it. The law applied the same to everyone.

Two horse thieves named Britt and Hilligoss stole some particularly valuable stock in Denver on one of the coldest days of winter, 1867. After following a mistaken lead north to Boulder on horseback, the marshal returned to Denver, picked up good information that showed the pair headed east, and having no one available to help him at the time, started after them by stagecoach. For a hundred and seventy-five miles he followed them along the main route into Kansas. All along the way he continued to get reports that made him confident he was catching up to the thieves. At Bijou, he changed out of his uniform and into clothing that would let him pass for a stage driver and rode up in the box with the regular driver. Well out of Colorado by late afternoon, they stopped at Sharon Springs, Kansas, and learned they were close on the heels of their prey. The two had stopped there to rest and water their horses.

As they continued east watching for the men, Cook instructed the driver to pass them with no sign of recognition, but when they were fifty yards or so beyond the outlaws he was to stop the coach suddenly and jump down cussing as if something had broken. When it happened, Dave climbed down beside the driver and kept his back to the outlaws. When he heard them come in close behind, he turned, gun in hand, and yelled, "Hands up!"

They were so astonished that they didn't move until he gave them the order again and cocked his pistol at the same time. He took their guns and walked them into nearby Fort Wallace and arranged for transportation back to Denver the next day. The only thing going that way was a closed freight wagon, and they were about as near to frostbite in it as they had been outside. Dave and the two horse thieves sat across from each other on the floor of the wagon all of that day and into the evening. Dave had been awake for almost four days and nights and was starting to doze off. He felt his gun moving in its holster. Britt was trying to slip it out with his feet. Cook slapped his hand down on his pistol.

"You don't want to live long, do you? One move out of you and I shoot. I sure hope you don't put me to the trouble of cleaning my gun. A lot of bother—cleaning a gun."

Then he relaxed back against the wall of the coach, and the outlaws concentrated on keeping still.

During Dave Cook's four years as town marshal of Denver, then several years as sheriff of Arapahoe County, he matched his guns and stamina against numerous "bad men." But those incidents are not what make him stand out in comparison to the average law enforcement officer of his time. He had the vision and organizational skills that led to the creation of the Rocky Mountain Detective Association. It was his understanding that led it from a civilian adjunct of official law enforcement to an organization that fostered close cooperation between official jurisdictions. Finally, he led it to its end as a crime fighting organization, supplanted by modern communications and more practical police methods. The most impressive part is that he foresaw and approved each step of that progression.

Dave Cook chose not to run for re-election as sheriff in 1879 and left office at the beginning of 1880. He was not idle. Some years before he had been made a major general in the Colorado Militia, and shortly after leaving office he was appointed as a special deputy United States marshal. His work as the head of the Detective Association also continued.

Unable, or unwilling, to deal with some emergencies without him, the governor called upon him to lead the troops he sent to Leadville to deal with a miner's strike during the summer of 1880. He was also to quiet the mobs and protect Chinese residents of Denver when the anti-Chinese riots broke out later that year. In both cases he was able to restore order. For the latter job the city fathers of Denver appointed him chief of police, and he held that job for a year.

He was an early believer in the developing methods of studying crime scenes and identification techniques and made frequent trips to larger cities in the Midwest, Chicago, St. Louis, and Cleveland to study the ways new police science was being applied in the large city forces. In his last years he reorganized the detective division of the Denver police force, and was still serving as a consultant for them almost until his death. As he grew older he felt he had accomplished those things that were his to do, and he began to withdraw. He was a man who avoided the glare of public attention, which explains why he is not better known.

General David J. Cook; law officer, detective, military leader, a man who made a difference; he was one of the "good guys."

Heck Thomas

For Duty and Adventure

Henry Andrew Thomas was known as "Heck" for nearly his entire life. The nickname was given to him by schoolmates as a boy. He was from a family with long roots in the history of America, but the tradition that pulled most at him was military service. One ancestor, General Leonard Covington, had served during the Revolutionary War. His uncle was General Edward Lloyd Thomas of the Army of the Confederate States of America, and Heck's father was a colonel in his brother's brigade. Colonel Thomas was badly wounded at Richmond and came home to recuperate. When he was able to return to his command in 1862, he took his twelve-year-old son, Heck, with him to serve as a courier. What could have been more exciting for a boy raised on martial traditions? He was going away to war. He wrote letters and proudly listed his return address as: Henry A. Thomas, Thirty-fifth regiment, Georgia volunteers, Thomas brigade, A. P. Hill's division, Stonewall Jackson's corps.

The most exciting event of his young life came when he was detailed to care for the horse and gear of fallen Union general Phil Kearny and then to take them through the lines under a flag of truce. General Lee had ordered that they be sent across so they could be returned to the widow.

Heck missed much of the latter part of the war. When he contracted typhoid fever, he was sent home to die. He managed not to do that, but by the time he was able to rejoin his father's regiment, Sherman's army had begun its advance toward Atlanta. Now war consisted of hardship and death. He saw plenty of both.

When the war was over, his family insisted on his resuming his education and wanted him to prepare for the ministry. He started school at Emory University, but studies did not suit him very well. When Heck was eighteen, Colonel Thomas was appointed city marshal of Atlanta, and the son once again joined his father. Heck became a city police officer. He served through some of the difficult years of Reconstruction, then at twenty-one he married Isabelle Gray, a minister's daughter in Atlanta, and they soon had two children.

The responsibilities of a family caused him to leave the police force in order to start a wholesale grocery business with two of his friends. That lasted for only a short time. Business life was indoors, restrictive, and predictable. None of that suited Heck Thomas, so he shortly moved his family to Texas.

They took the boat to Galveston to meet his cousin Jim. Jim Thomas had a job arranged for him. Heck became an express agent, like his cousin, for the Texas Express Company on the trains from Galveston on the Gulf Coast to Denison on the Red River and back. It was the kind of life he wanted.

One of his first introductions to the problems he might expect was Cousin Jim's description of the way train robbers had hit his train. When he held them off with gunfire, they had forced him out of the car by threatening to burn it down around his ears. Jim was a little miffed when Cousin Heck allowed that he didn't think he would have to give up the money if they tried that with him.

The robbery of Jim's train had taken place at Allen Station just a few miles north of Dallas. Only one member of the gang of robbers was captured. Heck put his plan into action when the others were not found.

The train was on its way south in the middle of the night when it pulled into the station in the little town of Hutchins ten miles south of Dallas. Heck was getting freight ready to unload at Hutchins, and the mail clerk was preparing a mail-bag to be dropped. When the clerk stepped to the door to toss out the mailbag he jumped back, slammed the door, and yelled a warning to Heck. He had seen the robbers on the station platform.

Heck could not shoot through the window of the car because the thieves were using the stationmaster, the porter, the fireman, and the engineer as cover. He blocked the door and got busy. When the outlaws yelled for him to open up, he called back a suggestion that they head directly for a distant place with a climate similar to Texas. A few volleys of rifle fire through the car had no effect so the bandits tried an axe on the car door. Heck put a stop to that project with a couple of shots fired through the door in the direction of the chopping sounds. All during this activity he had been making his preparations, and he was ready just in time.

A fire was started under the express car, and it began to fill with smoke. When he could stand it no more Heck surrendered. The leader of the outlaws jumped into the car with his pistol ready. He demanded to know how much money was in the safe. Heck told him they were carrying twenty thousand dollars. The bandit could not conceal his excitement as he ordered Heck to open the safe and put the money in a bag. Reluctantly and after another threat, the safe was opened and Heck started loading up the sack. First a bag of coins that clinked loudly as it went, then the various packets of cash, each one addressed to a different business, each one sealed with wax.

Heck was lined up with the rest of the captives, and two of the robbers went into the mail room side of the car to see what they could find. About that time another member of the train crew came back. He had slipped off the back of the train when he saw what was happening. He had found a shotgun and was putting it to work. The men under guard took cover under the platform, and Heck made a run for the engine where he knew the engineer and fireman kept a couple of six-guns. That try lasted only a second. The man left to guard them got off a shot at Heck that hit his cheek. The bullet cut to the bone then punched through the base of his neck. Heck abandoned that try and joined the others in the shelter of the platform.

Things were getting lively now. Some passengers had figured out what was going on and were taking shots anytime they could see someone moving. The outlaws decided to be satisfied with their haul; after all, twenty thousand was a fine chunk of money. They headed for other places as fast as they could ride.

The train crew got themselves organized and back on their way south. Heck tore off a shirtsleeve and did his best to stop the bleeding from his wounds. Over his objections they stopped down the tracks at Corsicana and had him treated by a doctor. He insisted on going on with the train to complete his run.

The Texas Express Company's superintendent, C. T. Campbell, met the train in Houston. It was not until Campbell came on board the train that Heck dug around in the cold ashes in the bottom of the express car stove and pulled out the packets of money. The outlaws had made away with fake packets Heck had been carrying just for that purpose ever since the robbery that had cleaned out the express safe on his cousin's run. The gang's total take was the eighty-nine dollars in the bag of coins.

They got the coins and the packets of paper. Heck got and distributed a detailed description of the leader of the train robbers. When the description reached Denton County sheriff W. F. Eagan it made him think of a hired man who had once worked for him. There had been some rumors about that man, too. The search was on for Sam Bass in north Texas. It would eventually involve over one hundred fifty men and take months.

As soon as Heck had recovered sufficiently, he was sent back to Dallas by the company to work with detectives Sam Finley and James Curry in the search for Bass. It was a cooperative effort of two county sheriffs with posses, the railroad and express company detectives, and a special detachment of Texas Rangers. The Rangers had been raised for this one task and were commanded by June Peak. The searchers first located the outlaws' hideout in the creek bottoms near Denton. They coordinated their efforts and moved in from three different directions. They did not manage to take him with that effort. He knew the country too well, but they drove him away from the area where he had friends and support. It was not long before the gang, made up of Bass, Seaborne Barnes, Jim Murphey, and one other man, were spotted on the trail south near Round Rock, north of the state capital in Austin. The Rangers were staying on the track with the help of an informer in the gang.

Bass had planned to hold up the Round Rock bank, and the outlaws were in town to look it over. Two local officers, not in on the plans to set up an ambush for the Bass gang, saw the bulges under the coats of Bass and Seaborne Barnes. They challenged them about complying with the ordinance against carrying weapons. That started the party. Bass and Barnes pulled their guns and killed the two lawmen; however, they both died in the shootout with the Rangers that followed. One other member of the gang escaped, left Texas, and was no longer a problem. The fourth man was Jim Murphey, the informant. He had made an excuse to hold back as they entered the town in order to avoid getting caught up in the shooting that he knew had to come.

Rewards were passed out, and the celebration was pretty general all over the state. Heck received a letter from the Texas Express Company in appreciation of his foresight and efforts in protecting the money being shipped on the night of the robbery. They were kind enough to enclose a check for two hundred dollars. That was not the end of the rewards for Heck's faithfulness and hard work. A few weeks later he was promoted to chief express agent in the Fort Worth office.

Fort Worth in 1879 was in the process of becoming a city. It was a center for western trade. Wholesale businesses thrived on the trains of freighters headed out to the western forts and communities. Cattle were still being driven to Fort Worth but no longer as a stop on the trail north. They were now being shipped out on the Texas and Pacific Railroad along with carloads of buffalo hides and bones—mountains of bones for the carbon plants in the East. It was still a place where the cowboys spent their "end of the trail" money. The last place to really cut loose.

The city had accommodated those needs for so long that the leaders saw it as their duty to keep the businesses thriving that gave so much pleasure to the cowboys. At the same time, of course, they made sure that a sizable chunk of the drover's pay was left in the pockets of those who provided the services. The section known as Hell's Half Acre was a booming, noisy, dangerous place that often managed to spill its problems over into the rest of the city.

Heck Thomas had made the acquaintance of the city marshal while he was out after the Bass gang. Timothy Isaiah "Longhair Jim" Courtright had been out after the same bunch for some stagecoach stickups in his jurisdiction. Heck learned a lot about police work from Courtright. Fortunately he didn't learn the man's rather flexible notions of right and wrong. Courtright's end came years later after he had left and returned to Fort Worth. He was operating a private detective agency, which was little more than a cover for a protection scheme. He was killed by gambler Luke Short in an argument over the payment of the "insurance" money.

Heck's job ended when the Texas Express Company folded under the competition from Wells, Fargo and Company and Pacific Express. He felt he had a real stake in the city becoming a decent place to live. His family had grown, and his wife was in a constant state of concern over raising the children in such a wild frontier place. It was easy to say "yes" when he was approached in 1885 to run for city marshal. Longhair Jim had left town; Heck had the popularity and, based on his experience as a policeman in Atlanta, the qualifications to be city marshal. The voters almost agreed, but he lost by only twenty-two votes.

With a growing family to feed, Heck looked for something to do that would bring in a living. So he started the Fort Worth Detective Agency and began to put to use some of the things he had learned.

Shortly after he opened for business he was approached by a local cattleman with a proposition. Alva Roff explained that two of his brothers, Jim and Andy, had been killed on their ranch up in the Chickasaw Nation of Indian Territory. The killers were a gang of thieves and murderers led by brothers Pink and Jim Lee. Roff was offering a reward of twenty-five hundred dollars each for the Lees, and the state of Texas would pay another thousand for their capture or death. The Lees lived in Indian Territory where Jim held land by virtue of his marriage to a Chickasaw woman, but their main business was crossing the Red River into north Texas and stealing livestock or anything else likely to show a profit.

The Roff brothers had lost some livestock to the Lees and joined a posse led by Sergeant James Guy of the Indian Police. As was common, Guy was also commissioned as a deputy U.S. marshal. The Lee brothers had steadfastly refused to abide by Chickasaw law, which forbade any citizen to fence more than six hundred and forty acres. He held a warrant for the Lees' arrest and orders to open up their fences. When the posse tried to take the gang at Jim Lee's place, Sergeant Guy, Jim and Andy Roff, and one of the Roff's riders, Billy Kirksley, were killed. Numerous posses and lawmen had gone looking for the outlaws but had succeeded only in burning down the deserted ranch house. The Lees had gone to cover.

After some serious thought, Heck decided to go after them. He was just getting his business started and could use the money. His wife realized this was going to be a particularly long and difficult trip and urged him not to leave her alone with the five children, in what she considered a wilderness outpost. Still, he decided the job was too important to turn down, and he had confidence in his ability to take care of himself. Isabelle would just have to care for the children and survive Fort Worth until he could return.

Heck knew the type of men he would be facing. He had known one of the gang members, Frank Pierce, who had called himself Frank P. Roberts when "Longhaired Jim" Courtright ran him out of Fort Worth. Thomas was not afraid of going up against men like that.

It was not a one-man job. Heck went to Indian Territory and looked up Jim Taylor. Taylor had been a deputy sheriff that Heck had become friendly with during layovers in Denison at the end of his express run. Now he was a deputy U.S. marshal working Indian Territory for the Parker court in Fort Smith, Arkansas. During this time federal deputies were paid fees, mileage, and expenses only, no salary. If they captured a criminal with a state, local, or private reward offered, they could claim that as well. They were federal employees so they were not entitled to claim any rewards offered by the United States government.

It was not just the reward that interested Taylor. The United States authorities now wanted the Lee brothers for the killing of a deputy marshal, Sergeant Guy, as well as the murders of non-Indians committed in Indian Territory. Those crimes had to be dealt with by the federal courts. Texas wanted them for various violations related to the business of stealing livestock in that state, and the Chickasaw courts wanted them for land violations. The brothers Lee were much wanted men.

The rewards offered for them were high enough to warrant a search that took two months. The plan was to wait to catch them when they crossed Red River on a raid and arrest them in Texas. The bandits would then be away from the area where they had friends and support, and the jurisdictional problems were lessened.

The two lawmen finally caught up with the Lees at day-break. The outlaws were on their way back to their hideout in Indian Territory when Taylor and Thomas spotted them. They let the brothers finish cutting their way through a fence. When they were about seventy-five yards away they stepped out of concealment with their rifles ready.

The Lees were not about to give up. They grabbed for their guns, but the two man-hunters fired at almost the same moment. Taylor's bullet cut Pink down before he could get into action. Jim got off three wild shots as he went down even after being shot in the neck by Heck. The two lawmen loaded up the bodies and hauled them in to Gainesville, the county seat of Cooke County, Texas, then turned them over to the local authorities and filed the claim for the rewards.

As a result of that affair, "Heck Thomas" became a name people knew. The story of the fight with the Lees leaped from the pages of the reports to the pages of the newspapers and on in rippling circles. One result was a flood of job offers. Back in Fort Worth, the Democratic Party leadership asked him to run on their ticket for Tarrant County sheriff. When he went to Austin to be presented the state reward money, the governor asked him to accept an appointment to the Texas Rangers, promising him rapid promotion. These offers did not really resolve the problem Heck faced. He had another plan.

After talking it over with Isabelle, the decision was made. He would apply for a commission as deputy United States marshal working out of the federal court in Fort Smith, Arkansas. They had heard that Fort Smith was a more established place, a small city with churches, schools, and a lack of the "wild west" atmosphere that kept Isabelle frightened and depressed.

He wrote a letter to the United States marshal for the western district of Arkansas asking for appointment as a deputy. He was quickly accepted and learned later that an unrequested recommendation from Jim Taylor had made it easy for him. The family was away to Fort Smith, Arkansas, where Heck served warrants in the Indian Territory for the court of His Honor, Judge Isaac Parker, the hanging judge.

Heck was out, sometimes for months at a time, on trips with the "tumbleweed" wagon, rounding up crooks in the Indian Nations. There have been few times and places where enforcing the law was as dangerous as it was for those federal officers. Isabelle waited during every trip wondering if she would get the notice that her husband had been killed.

Even Heck's attempt to give Isabelle some attention and a break from her responsibilities and loneliness failed miserably. They had taken a ride out from Fort Smith into the edge of Indian Territory. He stopped the buggy by a stream and unhitched the horses to let them drink and rest while the couple walked to the top of a hill to take in the view. As they returned, Heck saw a man preparing to steal their horses and shot him. He promptly handcuffed the wounded man and loaded him into the buggy. The pleasant drive in the country ended with delivering a cussing, bleeding, smelly horse thief to the jail in Fort Smith. The thief must have wondered about his luck in picking someone to rob. Isabelle's feelings about living on the frontier were only intensified.

Things were only to get worse. In 1887 the arrival of the railroads to the Chickasaw Nation in what is now south central Oklahoma brought a booming population and all of the attendant problems. The governor and the council of the Chickasaws requested the Court to station a resident deputy marshal in the Nation. The man who had done the most work in the area, who knew and was respected by most of the citizens, was Heck Thomas.

Heck was a brave man. He lived with danger and never succumbed to fear. Except this one time. He put off telling Isabelle about his impending transfer until it was too late. She saw it in the newspaper.

The new assignment took them to Whitebead Hill, Chickasaw Nation, Indian Territory. It was not like the open, rip-roaring Fort Worth, or the slightly better civilized but still upsettingly rough Fort Smith. This was a true primitive frontier community. There were a couple of stores, a boarding school for Indian children which whites could attend by paying tuition, and a very few other businesses. The only religious services were conducted by circuit preachers who came through on occasion. It was dirty, loud, and frightening. In the beginning she had to do the cooking in a pot over a fire in the yard. It is quite possible that the anxiety felt by the families of all peace officers both then and now had a part in her decision. Whatever the reasons, Isabelle returned to Georgia and divorced him.

It was a difficult time for Heck. After his wife left for Georgia he had to start moving three wagon loads of prisoners to Fort Smith. He had with him one of his favorite and most reliable possemen, Ed Stokely. He intended to recommend Stokely for appointment as a regular deputy. ·When they arrived at McAlester, Heck received word that his friend and fellow deputy Frank Dalton had been killed while he and another deputy, James Cole, were trying to arrest a man named Smith for horse theft and bringing alcoholic beverages into Indian Territory. They found Smith with his brother-in-law, Lee Dixon, Dixon's wife, and William Towerly. When they told them they had warrants for Smith the four opened fire. Smith shot Dalton in the chest, and he went down badly hurt. William Towerly, described as a "boy" horse thief, ran to Dalton, put the barrel of his rifle in the officer's mouth, and fired. He shot him once more in the head just to be sure.

There is no coincidence in finding that name on an Oklahoma lawman. Frank was a good officer, both in his skills and his commitment to duty. He was also the older brother of outlaws Emmitt, Bob, Grat, and Bill Dalton.

Cole, in the meantime, was being shot at by Smith, Dixon, and the woman. Cole was wounded in the side by Dixon but managed to kill his wife and Smith. Dixon was wounded badly enough that there was no fight left. The outlaw later died of his wounds in the jail hospital. William Towerly got away into the Choctaw Nation.

When Thomas received the notice of Dalton's death, he had a dilemma. He had two possemen, and they were holding seventeen prisoners. It had not been long since he had left his posse with prisoners to go after an outlaw. They had been ambushed and killed by friends of a prisoner. This time he sent Stokely and the other posseman, Bill Moody, after the killer, and he stayed with the seventeen prisoners.

The lawmen found Towerly at his parents' home. When they called to him to surrender, he went for his gun. Stokely shot him in the leg, and Moody hit him in the right shoulder. He dropped his gun as he fell, but as Stokely moved in to secure him, the boy grabbed the pistol with his left hand and shot him through the heart. Moody had his hands full with the rest of the family but was able to get free and kill young Towerly before he could fire on him again. They had tried to take him alive, and it cost Ed Stokely his life. It may have been reluctance to kill or it may have been the fact that the Court paid nothing for a dead body. The deputy and posse were only paid arrest fees and expenses for bringing in criminals who could be tried.

A year or so later, Heck discovered what a mixed lot luck can bring a man. He was out in the Creek Nation after a gang who had robbed a train. He had three posse members with him when they found the gang holed up on Snake Creek. They were hiding out at the site of a still operated by their leader, Aaron Purdy. The officers rode in, and Thomas ordered the men to drop their weapons. Purdy drew quickly and fired a couple of shots. Heck went down with a wound in his left side. Another bullet had broken his right wrist. The posse fired as one man, and Purdy died instantly. It was an effective lesson for the rest of the gang. They quickly gave up and were placed under arrest.

Heck was taken into Tulsa for medical attention. It was while he was recovering from his wounds that his luck turned. He met a schoolteacher named Matie Mowbray. They were married three years later, and Heck started his second family. Matie, like the first Mrs. Thomas, was a preacher's daughter but apparently made of sterner stuff.

While he was courting Matie, Heck was involved in another notable fight. He and possemen "Bones" Isbel, Dave Rusk, and a man named Salmon slipped up on a cabin located in thick woods southeast of Tahlequah in the Cherokee Nation. It was the home of Ned Christie, blacksmith, gunsmith, and sometime horse thief. Christie had been a member of the legislature of the Cherokee Nation until he killed an officer who tried to arrest him for "introducing" liquor into Indian Territory.

The posse moved in on Christie's cabin at first light but lost their chance to surprise the outlaw because of the warning set up by the watchdogs. Christie woke up and opened fire on the officers from the sleeping loft of the cabin. It was obvious that they couldn't get closer to the cabin so they had to find a way to bring Christie out. Heck set fire to the small workshop near the house, and when the fire spread to the house, things began to happen.

Christie spotted Isbel hiding behind a tree, and the deputy went down with a bullet through the shoulder. Christie's wife and a hired boy came out of the cabin and ran for the woods. Salmon and Rusk fired, seeing only fleeing bodies, and hit the boy in the hip and through the upper body.

Heck grabbed Isbel and pulled him into cover, and the other two officers joined them. As they cared for the downed deputy, Thomas saw Christie start out of the cabin to join his family. Heck fired once with his rifle, and the bullet hit Christie in the face. It shattered the bridge of his nose and destroyed his right eye. In spite of his wound, Christie made it to the trees and escaped.

Christie survived to rebuild, but this time he built what amounted to a small fort on a cliff about a mile from his burned-out cabin. It was two-logs thick and had gun slits for covering the entire area around the cabin. He had cleared out all of the brush and trees that could be used as cover to approach the house.

Several assaults were made and failed. Deputy Marshal Paden Tolbert led a fifteen-man posse equipped with a three-pound cannon. The cannon finally split after about thirty rounds, but the cannon balls just bounced off the stout walls of the fort anyway. The posse finally built a rolling shield from oak planks and the remains of an old wagon. During the night, they pushed their portable protection up to the wall as Christie and a friend fired on them. They placed a bundle of dynamite at the foot of the wall and headed quickly for cover.

The explosion blew open the wall and started a fire. Christie and his friend ran out and almost escaped, but Christie ran into posse member Wes Bowman in the thick smoke and missed his first shot. Bowman killed him as he turned to run.

Heck was involved in the hunt for both the Dalton and the Doolin gangs and ran down some of the remnants of both. It was the long search for the various members of the Doolin gang that caused the title of The Three Guardsmen to be given to Heck Thomas, Chris Madsen, and Bill Tilghman.

Bill Doolin had been a member of the Dalton outfit but had been cut out of the gang because he was considered dangerous and unreliable. When he put together his pack of train robbers, horse thieves, and cutthroats they were among the most successful and deadly the West ever experienced. They preyed on trains, banks, and express offices all over the Twin Territories. Their hit-and-run tactics and the fear they caused in the people living in the less populated areas where they hid out made information hard to come by for the law officers who chased them.

The times were unsettled. The 1890s were a period of explosion of population and constant friction between the last of the old "wild" West and the desire for a settled and peaceful place to raise families. Towns like Guthrie, Oklahoma City, Perry, and Woodward had to be slowly closed down from their "wide-open" beginnings.

Heck and Bill Tilghman were called on to put a lid on Perry. It had become an instant city on September 16, 1893. Thousands of people crowded into the half section (three hundred and twenty acres) set aside for the town site. By some estimates, there were twenty-five thousand of them by nightfall of that first day. Hotels, gambling houses, banks, saloons, restaurants, and bordellos all opened instantly in tents or plank shacks quickly thrown up and just as quickly opened for business. Heck had seen it all before. In Perry, they even called it the same thing as they had in Fort Worth, Texas. It was Hell's Half Acre.

In Perry, unlike the case in Texas, there was strong support for the maintenance of some civic control over the excesses. Thomas and Tilghman were known and respected, and just their presence was enough to make some malefactors look for more promising places to practice their various trades. However, as politics heated up and the money involved came more and more from the gambling and "entertainment" element, more conflict arose over just how efficiently the laws should be enforced. By this time Thomas and Tilghman were on the Perry City payroll and held their commissions from the Federal Court without pay.

With the help of Osage trackers Spotted Dog Eater and Howling Wolf, Thomas found "Little Bill" Raidler hiding out in a cave near Bartlesville. As the lawmen approached the cave, Raidler started shooting. Heck fired one time with his Winchester and hit Raidler in the hand. The outlaw ran into thick brush and got away. All they found were two fingers that he had cut off of the ruined hand. It remained for another of the "Guardsmen" to get the rest of "Little Bill." He was found later by a posse led by Bill Tilghman, who arrested what was left of him after a vicious fight that left Raidler with six bullet wounds.

About a year after the fight with Raidler, Heck led a posse that found Bill Doolin hiding out at his father-in-law's farm. They were hidden along the lane leading to the farmhouse when Doolin came along leading his horse. Heck called for Doolin to surrender, but the outlaw started firing with his Winchester. The posse returned fire, and a bullet hit Doolin's

Heck Thomas
(photo courtesy of University of Oklahoma Libraries)

rifle, knocking it from his hands. Not ready to give up, Bill pulled his six-gun and continued firing. Thomas and posse member Bill Dunn cut loose with their shotguns at the same time. Doolin was swept off his feet and died. They counted twenty-one bullet wounds in his body.

The Three Guardsmen went on to clean up the remnants of the Dalton and Doolin gangs. During the last hunts to finish up that chore that had lasted for years, Heck was assisted by "my best posseman, ever," his son Albert. They were together on the trail of Little Dick West, graduate of the Doolin gang and the only competent outlaw in that farcical "wild bunch" known as the Jennings gang.

It was a powerful posse consisting of Chief Deputy Marshal Bill Fossett, Lincoln County sheriff Frank Rinehart, Bill Tilghman, policeman Ben Miller, and Heck and Albert Thomas. They divided up to check out some houses. West saw Fossett and Rinehart coming and started shooting. They returned fire just as he was getting under a fence. West got up running and reloading, but about a hundred yards farther, when he stopped and turned to shoot again, Little Dick dropped dead. There would be plenty more crime in Oklahoma, and Heck Thomas was not through fighting it, but that was the end of the big organized gangs of train robbers.

In 1901 the U.S. marshal sent Heck to a new boomtown. What he had done in Perry and Whitebead Hill he was now to do in Lawton. That area of southwest Oklahoma Territory had just been opened, and Lawton was the new "wide-open" town.

Heck arranged with the county sheriff for an unpaid commission from the county to go with his credentials as a deputy U.S. marshal. Then he went about winning the support of the residents of the new town. His name and reputation were enough to get him a friendly hearing from the courts and the newly elected local officials. They agreed to the creation of a police force, and Thomas was elected chief. He started out with three police officers in a force that eventually grew to sixteen. He put them in uniform so the law would be visible, and soon things began to settle down.

He was chief of police for seven years, and near the end of that time some friends and admirers had a special badge made for him and presented it in a public ceremony. It was a gold star with a diamond in the center and had his name enameled in black on it. The Lawton paper wrote:

> Few men living have been presented a more beautiful emblem of esteem, and very few men could receive all the admiration and love that has been heaped upon him without getting the big head. . . Long may you live, friend Heck, and may the happiest days of your past be the saddest days of your future.

Heck was weakened by a severe heart attack and had barely recovered in time for the election of 1909. He could hardly campaign and did not win re-election. He was still not well but determined to be useful so he contacted the new U.S. marshal for the Western District of Oklahoma, Jack "Bring 'em Back Alive" Abernathy. He had been on the famous wolf hunt with Abernathy and Teddy Roosevelt in 1905, and Abernathy was glad to make him a deputy stationed at Lawton. By this time the deputy U.S. marshals were more process servers than outlaw catchers, but he enjoyed traveling through the southwest Oklahoma hills and valleys and often took his daughter Beth along with him in his buggy.

His old friend Chris Madsen became acting U.S. Marshal for the Western District at the end of 1911 and swore in his five deputies on New Year's night. Heck was there in Guthrie to be sworn in as one of them. Bill Tilghman came in from

Oklahoma City, and they made a reunion out of it. It wasn't to last. Heck's heart problem got worse, and by summer he was completely incapacitated. August 9 he wrote to Madsen: "...whatever happens don't you and Bill come down here, and no flowers...Remember me to your children, and good-bye forever. Your friend, Heck." A week later he was dead.

The notice was printed in the *Lawton Constitution* under this headline: "The Name of Heck Thomas, Once a Terror to Outlaws," and it might have added, one of the "Good Guys."

Grant Johnson
Quiet Law Enforcement

It was midafternoon in Eufaula, Indian Territory, 1901, when Frank Wilson and Wade Smith got into an argument on the street. Wilson ended the discussion by pulling a pistol and firing twice. He was not a very good shot. He missed both times and Smith got away. The shots were bound to attract the attention of law enforcement so Wilson headed out of town. He was not fast enough.

Deputy United States Marshal Grant Johnson mounted up and gave chase. He yelled for Wilson to stop and give himself up and punctuated his demand by firing into the air. When Wilson realized that he could not escape, he stopped and called back to the officer that he would "die before surrendering" and raised his pistol to take aim at the federal officer. Marshal Johnson fired first, and Wilson fell, gut shot. The deputy then had to get Smith under control. He had recovered from the fright of being shot at and gone hunting for a weapon. When he got his hands on a shotgun he returned to the street and wanted to finish off his assailant where he lay. Wilson was taken away for medical care but only lived until the next day.

The headline in the *Eufaula Indian Journal* read:

HIS FIRST KILL

Grant Johnson, Deputy Marshal,
Kills Frank Wilson

After describing the incident, the article finished with this paragraph:

> Grant Johnson has been a deputy United States marshal in these parts for fourteen years and has arrested more bad men than any officer in the Indian Territory. He has never before killed a man and has been forced to wound but one or two others. The people of Eufaula owe much to him for he has kept the peace in this town when the bad man was real bona fide bad man and numerous. His reward in cash has been slight. He has risked his life a hundred times in the interest of peace and held his hand when nine other officers out of ten would have killed. He has made no more than a living out of his office and the work is hard and dangerous. If merit can be rewarded among the deputies of the northern district, Johnson should be given a rewarding promotion of some sort for his fourteen years of hard service.

There was to be no such reward. Grant Johnson was a Creek freedman, a descendant of African slaves held by Creek Indian masters. He was almost certainly of mixed African-American and Native American blood, and no deputy of African ancestry was ever rewarded with an appointment to a higher position than that of deputy. This in spite of the fact that the records of service of men like Johnson and Bass Reeves were every bit as good as those of any others in the Indian Territory. In fact, it is unlikely that deputies in the

marshal's service with better records could be found anywhere in the West.

As is frequently the case with these lawmen, not much is
known about Johnson prior to the beginning of the official
records. His parents were Alex Johnson, a Chickasaw freedman and Miley, a Creek freedwoman. He is thought to have
been born somewhere in northeast Texas, but he began his
career as a deputy marshal about 1887 serving Judge Parker's
court in Fort Smith, Arkansas. In 1895 three federal districts
were created in Indian Territory, and Johnson was transferred
to the northern district to work out of the office in Eufaula. He
remained there for eleven years and gained the reputation
that led to the accolade quoted from the newspaper article..

While Grant Johnson was the victor in a number of gun
battles during his career, not every arrest required shooting.
Amos McIntosh, a member of the Creek Nation, killed Lee
Atkins, a Creek with a commission as a deputy U.S. marshal.
There was some delay in issuing an arrest warrant because
Atkins was not killed while carrying out his duties as a marshal. The question of which court had jurisdiction had to be
resolved. It was finally decided that the crime would be handled by the federal court at Fort Smith rather than the courts
of the Creek Nation, and Deputy Marshal Johnson was given
the writ to serve. Johnson decided there was no hurry.
McIntosh had been coming into town to shop regularly just as
he had before the killing. He would be back.

On a Monday in January of 1895 McIntosh was in Eufaula
in the Grayson Brothers general store when he was arrested
by Grant Johnson. McIntosh was completing the purchase of a
coffin and shroud. His wife had died the day before. The deputy took his prisoner back to the McIntosh home, and they
stayed there until after the funeral the next day. When the

service was over they headed to Fort Smith for the killer to face Judge Isaac Parker.

It was hardly one month later when Johnson was in Muskogee and spent a good while in casual conversation with an acquaintance, Wade Chamberlee, who had been arrested some time earlier. The grand jury had failed to find enough evidence to bring in an indictment in that case so he was released. What neither man knew at the time was that new evidence had come before the grand jury, and an indictment and warrant for arrest had been issued the day before. While still in town, Johnson was sought out by another deputy, George Lawson, who asked if he knew the wanted man well enough to point him out. While they worked on getting their laughter under control, the two officers went to the saloon where Chamberlee was having a drink and took him into custody. Wade Chamberlee may not have found the circumstances quite so amusing.

Grant Johnson occasionally worked with Bass Reeves, the great African-American deputy marshal whose career spanned the entire period of federal court jurisdiction over law enforcement in the Indian Territory. Johnson was involved, along with Reeves, in the arrest of one Abner Brasfield early in 1890. They had a warrant for Brasfield for a murder committed in Arkansas before his family relocated to the Territory. Along with the warrant came the promise of a $1,500 reward.

They brought him in handcuffed to his saddle with his feet shackled to a chain that went beneath the horse. On the way to town they stopped by the Brasfield place to let the family know that Abner was in custody and was being returned to the state where the crime was committed. When they got to Eufaula they turned him over to the temporary custody of a local law officer named Andy Duren so they could get some breakfast.

Brasfield was allowed off the horse with the chain still shackled to one ankle and the handcuffs on one wrist. Several of the family had followed the trio into town, and when a cousin stepped off his horse he let it walk on up by Brasfield. Abner knew what he was looking for when he reached in the saddlebag. He came up with a Colt six-shooter and threw down on Duren. When Duren drew and shot too quickly for accuracy, Brasfield fired and wounded him in the hand. The street cleared and Brasfield "lit a shuck."

The two deputies heard the shooting and dropped their search for a morning meal. They were too late to catch Abner and had to settle for arresting the Brasfield cousin and Abner's father for aiding a federal prisoner to escape. Those two were taken to Fort Smith where they posted bond, and after several trips for trial, the charges were eventually dropped.

Abner Brasfield took off for Texas and was gone for two years. After an encounter with a detective in Texas left him with an arm broken by a bullet, Abner seems to have considered the direction his life was going and decided to make a change. He returned to Eufaula and surrendered to Grant Johnson and was tried and convicted in Arkansas.

Late in 1900 Abner Brasfield's name figures in one of Grant Johnson's most spectacular exploits in a minor way but one that is revealing of the nature of the times. The following information comes from an article that appeared in the *Eufaula Indian Times* with the headline: John Tiger Goes To War.

Around midday on Christmas of 1900 John Tiger, a Creek Indian, and his wife came into town in their buggy. Tiger had apparently been availing himself of the opportunity to celebrate the season since it was just lunchtime and he was already well under the influence of something alcoholic. He got out of the buggy and walked down the street to a group of people who were visiting outside the Sorbe Restaurant. He had some words with a man named L. B. Roper. After a little conversation, the subject of which no one now recalls, Roper snatched a fence picket out of Tiger's hand and hit him over the head with it. The light piece of wood apparently did little damage and Tiger just said, "That is all right" and walked away.

Tiger returned to his buggy and after a short struggle with his wife managed to get a pistol from a bag and started back up the street. He first pointed his gun at a man named Bumgarner and called him Roper. Bumgarner threw up his hands and told him that he was not Roper just, "old Bill Bumgarner, your friend, John." So the intoxicated man turned away and shot Dave Porter in the back. He had evidently decided that he was going to keep shooting people until he got the right man.

The next to catch his attention was an old man on his way to the cafe. Tiger shot him through the head. Tiger then let off a few shots at a surveyor named Clemons, who ran and dodged so well and stumbled so fortuitously that he escaped with holes only in his pants leg and his dignity. When he fell, Tiger thought he was done with him so he next shot Jesse Beck through the body just above the hips. Tiger ran out of ammunition after inflicting one more wound, a minor one to the thigh of Buddy Taylor.

He headed for his place out of town to the east as fast as he could. He was trying to reload as he ran. He was hardly to the edge of town when Deputy U.S. Marshal Johnson was on his trail with the assistance of one Abner Brasfield as posse. The two officers caught up with the shooter. When he realized he would not get away he fired twice at Johnson but missed with both shots. While he was getting off those shots the deputy fired once and shattered the bone in Tiger's left arm. Since he had only managed to load those two bullets in his six-shooter and now was empty as well as wounded, Tiger threw the gun away as Johnson ordered.

The "badman" was patched up by the doctor in Eufaula, and Marshal Johnson delivered him to the court in Muskogee on the afternoon train. Before they left, there was talk of applying some summary, local justice in order to salve the feelings of the townspeople and save the government the cost of train tickets and a trial. Some of the calmer residents talked that idea down, and John Tiger was delivered safely to jail.

The Abner Brasfield who served as posse in this incident was the same man who had been arrested ten years before by Johnson and Bass Reeves. He had been pardoned by the governor on the murder conviction in Arkansas. After he returned to Indian Territory, he served several years on the Eufaula police force.

About a month later the Eufaula newspaper ran the following:

> The people of Eufaula made a purse a few days since and sent it to Grant Johnson as a mark of their appreciation of the prompt and courageous manner in which he arrested John Tiger on Christmas day. They also appreciated his effective work in preserving the public peace during the excitement that followed the lamentable occurrences of that day. A man cannot be paid in cash for this kind of work. Duty is all that prompts a man under such circumstances. This present to Grant is not, therefore, a reward but a mark of

appreciation of duty well done the reward for which is only the sense [of] duty well done.

Considering the racial climate of those times, this must be considered a real accolade. The man had obviously made an impact on the life of a community, and that community did not forget him.

This was a busy period for Grant Johnson. Along with everything else that occurred in his jurisdiction, a group of several hundred Creeks, who became known as the Snake faction, or "disaffected" Creeks, began a protest against the federally ordered breakup of the Creek Nation and the allotment of its lands to individual members of the tribe. They assembled and elected leaders, a bicameral legislature, and established a court. They declared the old laws of the Creek Nation to be still in force and organized a police force to enforce those laws. The police were given the task of gathering up those allotment certificates that had already been issued and making sure that no Creeks were employing or renting land to nonmembers of the Nation.

The Eighth Cavalry was eventually sent in to create enough of a federal presence to impress peace on the area, but the movement did not slow down until the arrest of its leaders. There are several news reports in the *Eufaula Indian Journal* about the arrest of Chitto Harjo, also known as Crazy Snake, the primary leader of the group, by "deputy marshal Grant Johnson and his posse." Harjo, along with eleven other of the leaders of the faction, was arrested by Johnson and jailed in Muskogee to be dealt with by the federal court there. The problems with members of this group continued until well after statehood when the Oklahoma National Guard was called out to settle things. Until 1905 there are still news reports of arrests of "Snake" Indians by Marshal Johnson.

Besides his work with Bass Reeves, Grant Johnson also did field work from time to time with James Franklin "Bud" Ledbetter. Ledbetter is another great peace officer of that time and area who served in many different capacities, but in the early years of the twentieth century he was a deputy U.S. marshal working out of Muskogee. Since the two towns were little more than thirty miles apart and on the same rail line, opportunities to cooperate must have been fairly frequent.

Late in 1904 a deputy marshal named Fink was on the trail of a couple of outlaws for the crime of "introducing," that is bringing liquor into the Territory. When he caught up with his quarry, he told them they were under arrest. One of the criminals, Jim Tiger, turned in his saddle and fired, killing the officer with one shot. Tiger and his partner, a man known only as "Fish," were soon the object of a manhunt involving over a hundred deputies. The deputies spread out over the area and arrested any pair of Indian men who resembled the description they had.

Johnson and Ledbetter finally captured the two and separated them. They each told one of the men that the other had confessed to being involved but named the partner as the one who killed Marshal Fink. The stories that poured forth then were sufficient to take them both to trial in the federal court at Muskogee.

While they had worked well together over several years, something happened after 1904 that strained that relationship, some conflict that caused bad feelings between the two men. Not all of what occurred is known, but one of the incidents that reveal animosity occurred when Ledbetter decided Johnson was not taking efficient enough action against the traffic in alcohol in the Eufaula area. Ledbetter made up his mind to do something about the situation and made a trip to

Eufaula without letting anyone, including Johnson, know he was coming. He came into town, raided several drugstores for selling liquor, destroyed their supplies of illegal booze, and placed several men under arrest for gambling.

He filed his report and made his way back to Muskogee, satisfied that he had corrected a problem of lax enforcement. As might be expected, this did not sit well with the proud officer who had been taking care of law enforcement in Eufaula for almost twenty years. Grant Johnson was not the kind of man to accept that kind of treatment without protest of some sort. It started the afternoon of the same day.

Johnson caught the afternoon train to Muskogee. He moved quietly around town spotting what was going on, and that night he raided gambling places, broke up four crap games, and arrested a dozen men. He didn't overlook the drugstores, those famous purveyors of "medicinal" but illegal whiskey. He destroyed the liquor supplies at several, made his report, and returned to Eufaula.

Deputy marshals assigned to different areas commonly were understood to be responsible for law enforcement in their area. The original purpose for a federal force was to eliminate the problems of jurisdiction, which occurred when a sheriff could not cross his county line or a town officer could not make arrests outside the city limits. Each federal deputy marshal had the authority to uphold the law and arrest lawbreakers in any jurisdiction.

There is no record of better relations being restored between the two men, and early in 1906 Marshal Leo Bennett of the Northern District of Indian Territory informed Grant Johnson that his commission as deputy United States marshal would not be renewed. It is possible that this resulted from Ledbetter's recommendation to the marshal. Nothing in the history of these men points to the estrangement having any core of racial prejudice, and Ledbetter remained close to Bass Reeves, another deputy of African-American descent, until Reeves' death. These were both proud, bold men with the strong convictions and stern self-confidence necessary to stand against the lawbreakers of their time. It seems likely that once a conflict started between two men of that disposition neither could back down.

Thus ended Grant Johnson's career in the federal service but not his life in law enforcement nor his connection with Eufaula, by then, the state of Oklahoma. He worked for a number of years for the city as a police officer, patrolling the African-American part of town with the same quiet strength of character and the same dignity that had marked all the rest of his career.

The last known newspaper mention of Grant comes from the *Muskogee Times-Democrat* of October 4, 1909:

Knife Used on Grant Johnson

an Old Deputy Marshal at Eufaula

Eufaula, Okla., Oct. 4.—(Special)—Grant Johnson, for many years a deputy United States marshal, and a good one, was badly wounded at Bond Switch by being stabbed in the neck by Robert Watson. Johnson is now at his home east of Eufaula and Watson is in jail awaiting the outcome of the wound.

Grant Johnson didn't die from that wound. He lived on to patrol the streets of Eufaula, be an example and inspiration for the young people of the community, and to instill in others his own sense of the importance of performing one's duty. It worked, at least for one. It led his only child, a son, John, to promotion and honor in the United States Army. John earned a Purple Heart in France during World War I, and when he was discharged he held the rank of staff sergeant.

Grant Johnson died April 9, 1929 and was buried in the African-American cemetery near Eufaula. He is not well remembered now, but he deserves to be. He should be remembered as one of the "good guys."

Bud Ledbetter
Many Badges, One Goal

James Franklin Ledbetter was new to the area of Coal Hill in Johnson County, Arkansas. He had recently taken up farming land not too far from the booming mining town and was making his first trip in to buy supplies. He was dressed for town in a white linen suit, and while the store got his order made up he thought he would have a look around this new place. He didn't drink, but there were a lot of saloons and not much else to see in Coal Hill so he stopped in one. His clothing gave a great deal of amusement to the working men who were enjoying a few afternoon drinks. They gathered around him and marveled over the suit, pulled out his shirttail, and had, in general, a very entertaining time. Bud, as he was called by those who knew him, was not enjoying the play nearly as much as his tormentors.

He never spoke. His face frozen, he walked out of the saloon. At least by that point the size and build of the man they were "hoorawing" should have made an impression even on whiskey befuddled brains. It was not far down the street to the hardware store where he went in and bought a large ax handle. When he reentered the bar he locked the door behind him.

Citizens on the street heard the noise and couldn't get in the building to see what was happening so they went for the mayor. When he arrived it was quiet inside, but the door was still locked. The mayor, with the help of some of the gathering crowd, forced the door open to find a good half dozen would-be tough guys lying around on the floor in various stages of unconsciousness. "Bud" Ledbetter was leaning on the bar with his ax handle still in his hand and his eyes cold and hard. He greeted the newcomers with, "What are you going to do about it?" At that point he was apparently ready to take on anyone or everyone.

What the mayor was going to do about it was to get the unconscious and wounded drug out of the saloon and have a little visit with the only man left standing. By the time that conversation ended, Coal Hill had a new city marshal. In the past they had had little luck in finding one and none at all in keeping one. They had one now who would stay as long as he decided to.

Ledbetter's first effort was to crack down on raucous behavior on the streets and in the public places of Coal Hill. He got warrants and started shutting down anyplace that was operating outside the law. Some of them were able to reopen when they agreed to strict standards for running their businesses. Quiet came to the streets as the miners found that bad behavior was met with consistent reaction from the marshal.

He had plenty of skill with weapons. He had been raised in the mountains where he was expected to help provide meat for the table from an early age. These skills were not much needed in this job, however. He made a few demonstrations under the guise of practice. Once he had busted a few shot glasses sitting on fence posts at twenty paces while shooting from the hip, word got around. He generally only found it necessary to "dent" the head of any man who resisted his invitation to "sleep it off" in the city jail.

Bud had been married since June of 1874. He and his wife, Mary Josephine, had a son, George W., who was five and a two-year-old daughter named America Jane but called "Dolly." There is no doubt that one of the standards he sought for the community was that it be a safe place for families like his own to live and grow. The town settled down. It didn't have much choice with Bud on the job. He and the family were happy in Coal Hill. It seemed like a place to stay, but it didn't last.

E. T. McConnell was the sheriff of Johnson County, and it wasn't long before he heard about what was happening in Coal Hill. He saddled up to go meet the man who had tamed the town. It did not take the astute sheriff long to size up the tall young man who had cooled off Coal Hill. It only took a moment longer to offer Bud a job as a county deputy. Ledbetter's hesitation to relocate evaporated in the face of an offer that doubled the pay he was making. He could not turn that down. They moved to Clarksville.

Bud served fourteen years as a Johnson County deputy sheriff, under three sheriffs, with nothing but the best said of him and his work. He also made friends that he kept for the rest of his life or theirs.

His first working partner and the one who exposed him to the ways of an investigator was longtime deputy John Powers. Powers would eventually be the sheriff, but for the first years of their working together the two became legend in the minds of the lawbreakers of the county. They were the Johnson County Invincibles.

When four local men tried to rob a train in nearby Franklin County, they not only killed the conductor and wounded a brakeman, they somehow managed to shoot one of their own number in the leg and the side. That pretty well broke up the attempt to stick up the train, and the gang made their getaway. When the news came over the telegraph for Sheriff McConnell, he immediately dispatched the "Invincibles" along with posseman Paden Tolbert to give any assistance possible to the sheriff in the neighboring jurisdiction. Tolbert was a young man who had studied to be a teacher but found that life dull in comparison to chasing criminals. He was well trained by Sheriff McConnell and was ready to go anytime volunteers were needed.

The three took the next train and were at the site of the holdup within an hour. They quickly found the wounded man concealed in the brush and abandoned by his partners. He would not, however, give the lawmen any information that would help to identify or catch the other outlaws.

They found the spot where the bandits had hidden their horses for the escape. It was clear that the trail was going to lead into the mountains to the north. The three officers secured a pack mule and a load of supplies, sent word to their boss that they might be "on the scout" for a while, and headed out. They were after three men who may not have been skilled in the business of robbing trains, but now they were wanted for murder and were not going to give in easily.

For three weeks they chased the men through the mountains, up one ridge and down the other, back and forth. Whenever he had the chance, Paden Tolbert sent word of their progress to his father, the owner of the *Clarksville County Herald*. That news was then reported in the paper so the community could keep up.

The three outlaws were finally run down and cornered. There was no fight left in them, and the deputies arrested them without incident. The officers brought them into the jail at Ozark, where their wounded companion was being held. One of the weary would-be train robbers told the crowd, "Them bastards would have followed us to hell, if necessary."

By 1890 progress and efficient law enforcement had brought a level of quiet to Johnson County that was making Paden Tolbert restless. By that time the young man was a deputy sheriff and one of Bud's closest friends. Tolbert looked west, into Indian Territory, where lawlessness still ran rampant and there was a need for officers who were not afraid to go after the criminals. It was in midyear 1891 that he accepted a commission as a deputy United States marshal for the federal court of the Northern District of Indian Territory and was assigned to work out of Vinita, Cherokee Nation.

For the next two and a half years letters came to the Ledbetter home from Paden. He wrote constantly of the excitement and opportunities that were available in "the Nations." Finally Bud had to go look for himself.

A stop in Fort Smith got Ledbetter a job offer before he even made it to Indian Territory. His reputation was already known, and Col. George Crump, the U.S. marshal of the western district of Arkansas, wanted Bud to become one of his deputies, serving writs and warrants in Judge Parker's jurisdiction. Bud wanted to look around first; he had started out to visit Paden Tolbert, and that is what he intended to do.

When Bud got to Vinita, Indian Territory, he found a place he thought he would like to live and raise his family. He and Tolbert visited and talked about the future. There were no current opportunities for a federal appointment, but Paden urged his friend to talk to the railroad. The express cars on the trains generally carried guards, sometimes deputy federal marshals who took the assignments to earn extra money. That sounded like the kind of life Bud was looking for so he applied for a job with the American Express Company whose cars were moved on the Katy line. He returned to Arkansas to close out his business there and get his family moved.

On the way back to Vinita to take up his new post, he stopped in Fort Smith once again to visit an old friend, Tom Isom. While he was there a man named Joe McNally managed to cause a delay for Ledbetter's first trip as an express guard.

McNally was known as a peaceful man when sober, but he wasn't in that condition quite often enough. He had shot a peace officer named Wiley Cox in 1890 while in a drunken state and was charged with assault. When Cox died of his wound in 1891 the charge was upgraded to murder. Now, in the summer of 1894, his lawyers were still managing to keep him out of jail and untried.

Ledbetter, Isom, and another friend named Morrow were celebrating their reunion in Doc Roger's saloon when they ran into McNally and a friend of his named Gardenhire. Isom and Gardenhire resumed an old quarrel, resulting in a round of fisticuffs which Morrow and Ledbetter broke up. In the process, McNally drew a gun and fired a round that did no damage. A local officer took his pistol and told the two battlers to "call it a night."

After Ledbetter and Morrow had delivered Tom Isom to his bed, Morrow decided that he would have one more drink. Bud went along for the company although he didn't drink alcoholic beverages himself. When they entered Doc Roger's place they were surprised to find that McNally had returned and started drinking again. Not only that, but he had also rearmed himself.

As soon as they came through the door, McNally drew. Ledbetter slowly backed toward the door, and just as he stepped down on the doorstep, his opponent fired. In almost the same instant, Ledbetter drew and fired his own pistol. McNally's bullet found the doorframe but missed his man. Ledbetter's was dead center, and the bad man was dead within minutes.

Bud Ledbetter waited at the marshal's office and turned himself in when it opened. It took a few days, but the court ruled that the shooting was justified. Bud was soon on his way to Vinita and his new job.

The life of an express guard was pretty boring until November 13, 1894. As the Katy *Flyer*, bound north from Dallas and carrying sixty thousand dollars in the safe, passed Muskogee and approached a siding known as Blackstone Switch, there was a gang waiting for it. They were a rough bunch. Led by Nathaniel Reed, known as "Texas Jack," the group included Tom Root, Buz Luckey, and Will Smith. The four had what seemed to them to be a foolproof plan. They would throw the "switch," shunting the *Flyer* off the main track onto the siding, and demand entrance to the express car. If the guards refused, the bandits would blow the car up with dynamite.

The train stopped as soon as the engineer saw the signal telling him the switch had been thrown, and the train robbers announced their intentions. Not getting what they wanted, they opened fire on the express car, shooting holes all through it. That, they thought, should convince the express messenger and the guards of the necessity of surrender. They had reckoned without the quality of men holding the express car. Their bullets were answered by a barrage of fire from the weapons of Bud Ledbetter, Deputy Marshal Paden Tolbert, and posseman Sid Johnson. Their terms of surrender rejected, the outlaws upped the ante. Reed threw some dynamite under the train car and blew part of the end out of the car as well as taking off part of the door. The defenders, however, were unhurt and kept up such a steady hail of bullets that the bandits were discouraged from making any further try on the express box.

If they were going to have to give up on the big payoff, at least they would take what they could get. Reed told his men to keep up a steady fire on the express car while he checked the passengers for contributions in order to salvage some profit out of their work. He made his way to the smoker at the end of the train and invited a couple of passengers to assist him by passing around a cloth bag and collecting up all cash, watches, and jewelry. According to Reed, in a later account, no doubt well embellished over the years, the collection netted six hundred and forty dollars, eight watches, and three pistols.

Settling for that tidbit in exchange for the expected treasure of sixty thousand in cash was not enough humiliation. As Reed made his way back to his companions, he came into Ledbetter's sights for only a moment through a crack in the end of the express car. It was all Ledbetter needed. A quick shot hit Reed in the hip and passed through his lower body. When he fell Buz Luckey ran to him, picked him up, and the four outlaws made their escape. Once they were well away from the railroad, Reed had them make him a bed in the shelter of some rocks, gave them each a watch and a little money from the sack, and told them to get away. All he asked was that when things cooled off enough, they try to come back and bury his body. He was convinced by that point he was dying.

When they came back the next day to bury him, he was not yet dead so they brought him some food and supplies and doctored him the best they could. They cared for him for three days until they spotted deputy marshals and Indian

Lighthorse police searching for them. Reed again told them to leave him and make their way to safety. After another day and a half he was strong enough to get up and hobble several miles to the home of Tom Root's sister. She hid him and cared for him until he was able to travel by wagon and then they took him first to Missouri, then to his brother's place in the Boston Mountains of Arkansas.

This experience gave Texas Jack Reed a change of heart about the life he was living, and he wrote to Judge Parker at Fort Smith a few months later to tell him where to send officers to get him. He was arrested and transferred to the prison hospital and indicted. He confessed to the Blackstone Switch robbery and agreed to testify against Luckey, Root, Will Smith, and Jim Dyer, a local rancher that Reed accused of being the mastermind of the attack. He claimed that Dyer recruited them and worked out the plan then failed to appear as agreed when the time came.

All five were sentenced to prison, with Dyer's conviction being eventually overturned on appeal. Reed, as agreed in his plea bargain, was placed on probation for five years. He served out his probation in Arizona, reporting faithfully as instructed. When he successfully completed the five years without getting into trouble, he was given a pardon. He became an itinerant preacher and evangelist and traveled the country using his own life as the example of the results of evil living. His record of evil acts was somewhat exaggerated for effect, but he sold his message and his story for the rest of his life. He died in Tulsa in 1950.

In later years when Ledbetter was reminded of the fight at Blackstone Switch or he saw a report of Reed's travels, he said. "I saw him 'hunkering' for them crossties with the sack of loot, and let him have it. That shot made a preacher out of him."

The outlaws of the Nations were beginning to have the same sort of respect for Bud Ledbetter as those in Arkansas who had known him as one of the "Invincibles." An incident in 1895 shows that it was not only the bad guys who were impressed. The Rufus Buck gang had been terrorizing the Creek Nation and the general vicinity for months when they went on a wild two-week rampage of robbery, murder, and rape.

The brutality of the crimes committed by Buck, Sam Sampson, Louis Davis, Maoma July, and Lucky Davis aroused a high level of indignation in the citizens of the Creek Nation as well as all the varied law enforcement agencies with jurisdiction in the area. Captain Edmund Harry of the Creek Lighthorse police with a group of his men was after the gang. There were deputy U.S. marshals in the field hunting them. Groups of armed Creek citizens were searching the countryside. With this much attention it is no surprise that the five members of the gang were finally spotted. They were discovered camped in some trees on top of a steep hill known locally as "Flat Rock."

Captain Harry and his men, accompanied by marshals Samuel Haynes and N. B. Irwin, surrounded the hill. The gang was in a good position. They had cover while the attackers were at the bottom of a bare, steep slope with only the protection of the tall grass. Creek citizens joined them until the number rose to about a hundred besieging the hill. The firing was so constant that it sounded like one steady roar, and the smoke from the black powder cartridges hung so heavy that neither side could see well enough to get in a good shot at the other. Finally, an old Creek in the posse reached the end of his patience. He stood up from the grass at the bottom of the hill and announced, "Let us stand up and fight like men; I'm tired of this."

Unfortunately, this brave man's name has disappeared like the smoke of the battle. He started up the hill and fired a round at Rufus Buck, who was hiding behind a tree. The bullet hit the tree, but a fragment clipped Buck's belt, startling him, and he dropped his rifle and ran. The posse followed the old man, and the outlaws followed their leader. Soon three of the gang were in custody. Louis Davis and Sam Sampson escaped in the confusion. Sampson, with the help of his family, turned himself in to the officers before they got back to town with the other prisoners.

Lynching talk started as soon as people knew the men had been captured. The marshal quickly assembled his officers. He stationed Bud Ledbetter and Paden Tolbert, who had just missed the fight at Flat Rock, at the gate into the jail yard. When the crowd gathered, the marshal climbed up on a wagon and had a talk with them. He made all the expected arguments for letting the law do its job. He reminded them of the record of Judge Parker, in Fort Smith, who would sit in judgement and pass sentence on the bloody foursome.

With each point the crowd seemed to settle and then quickly arouse itself to the boil again. Finally, the marshal pointed out the guards at the gate. There stood Ledbetter and Tolbert, Winchesters in their hands, ready for whatever came next. The only argument that seemed to have any effect was when the marshal reminded them that, while they could probably take the prisoners by force of numbers, Ledbetter and Tolbert would not sell their lives cheaply. They would do their duty and take quite a few of the mob with them into the great beyond. That message seemed to get through; the deputies were respected for their integrity and courage as well as their skills. No one wished the officers any harm, and no one seemed inspired to step up and be the first to die in the attempt to administer tree limb justice.

The next day the prisoners were slipped quietly out of town and taken to the federal jail at Muskogee to await transport to Fort Smith for their date to stand before the bench of Isaac Parker, the "hangin'" judge. A few months later the judge lived up to his nickname, and Buck, Davis, July, and Sampson stepped up on the gallows and dropped through the trap simultaneously. They had been saved for their official moment of justice by the courage and reputations of two of the "good guys."

The Jennings family were early settlers of Oklahoma Territory. The father, J. D. F. Jennings, claimed a quarter section near Kingfisher in the Run for the Unassigned Lands in 1889. Jennings, who was a former Methodist minister and a surgeon, had taken up the practice of law after the Civil War and had followed the frontier west. He had ended up in Colorado before making the Run. His sons Ed, John, and Al had followed him into the profession, and by 1892 all four were practicing law in Oklahoma Territory. Another son, Frank, had stayed behind in Colorado.

In 1893 a Land Run opened the Cherokee Outlet in the northwestern part of Oklahoma Territory. The senior lawyer Jennings was appointed judge of the probate court in Woodward, the seat of the county of the same name. By 1894 the three Jennings sons who were in Oklahoma had all moved their practice to Woodward, as well. This move set in motion the events that eventually created, what surely must be, the most inept band of outlaws the West ever saw.

The Jennings brothers came into conflict over court cases with one of the truly colorful characters of the time. Temple Houston, the youngest son of old General Sam Houston, of Tennessee and Texas, had been one of the early settlers of Woodward and probably the best known. He was quick witted, quick tongued, quick tempered, and just as quick with his gun. A confrontation in court led John Jennings and Houston to the point of drawing on each other. They were restrained by other members of the court and soundly dressed down by the judge. The dispute started again when Ed and John Jennings and Temple Houston happened to meet in the Cabinet Saloon that evening. A shootout followed that left John dead and Ed severely wounded.

The evidence, however, seemed to show that the bullet that had killed John had come from Ed's gun when his arm was hit by a bullet probably fired by Houston. This being the case, Houston was acquitted, and Al Jennings and another brother, Frank, who had remained on his job in Denver when the family moved, went "on the scout," making plans to get the family's revenge on Temple Houston. While they talked a lot about what they were going to do "when they found Houston," Temple never changed his routine, and the two would-be feudists never managed to "catch up" with him. They never "looked" for him in Woodward where he continued to live and work without seeming to take any notice of their threats.

Al and Frank were usually to be found more than two hundred miles to the east in Indian Territory in the company of a pair of brothers named O'Malley. When they ran out of money, their friends helped them get jobs as ranch hands on the Spike S in the Creek Nation. It was there, probably in early 1897, that the two pairs of brothers met a real outlaw. Little Dick West had ridden with the Doolin gang and since the death of

Bill Doolin had been lying low in the Creek country. With West as their leader, the five set out to make their way in a life of outlawry.

In June of the same year, Bud Ledbetter was sent to investigate the robbery of a store and post office southeast of Vinita, Indian Territory. The bandits had come in disguise, used a special tool to pull the lock out of the safe, and got away with seven hundred dollars. Behind the false facial hair, the postmaster recognized Al Jennings. It was a warm-up to make sure the tool worked and get some spending money to move on into the big jobs. Bud went after them, but they stayed on the move and he could never catch them.

It was mid-August when the gang tackled their first big job. They took over a train during the night at a water stop near Edmond just north of Oklahoma City. They forced their way into the baggage car but were not able to get the safe open. They even tried dynamite. It caused a good deal of damage but not to the safe. They had to give up and run back to cover in the Creek Nation.

They were not out of action for long. Having eluded pursuit once again they planned another job. This time they worked out a foolproof way to rob the Katy train at Bond Switch. They took a bunch of railroad ties they found along the right-of-way and stacked them on the tracks. When the train was heard approaching, they set the ties on fire and got ready to make their haul. The engineer, who recognized immediately what was going on and knew the capabilities and limits of his equipment, simply opened the throttle and left the boys standing amidst a scattered bunch of flaming timbers, gawking at the rapidly disappearing train.

The would-be train robbers still managed to stay ahead of Ledbetter, but by this time he had discovered where they went to ground. He convinced Sam Baker and Willis Brooks, a couple of the men who had been putting the gang up between jobs, that it would be a good idea to get word to the law the next time the five showed up. His argument was persuasive since both Bud and the newly recruited informers knew that Baker and Brooks had backgrounds of their own that would not stand the scrutiny of the law.

In the meanwhile the gang had moved to the western edge of Indian Territory with the plan to take a ninety-thousand-dollar express shipment from a Rock Island train headed to Fort Worth, Texas. They took over a section house north of Chickasha and forced the crew to flag down the train. Pat O'Malley and Frank Jennings held the passengers and conductor while Al Jennings and West broke into the express car. They found a small safe and a large one, both billed through to Fort Worth. They had brought dynamite once again—probably furnished themselves with a good deal more than they had used at Edmond. They put the explosive on top of the large safe and then set the smaller one on top of that. They lit the fuse and took cover.

The explosion blew a hole in the side of the train car and threw the small safe completely out into the railroad right-of-way. Neither safe, however, sustained any serious damage. They had to content themselves with the conductor's silver watch and whatever cash they could take from the passengers. It amounted to about three hundred dollars.

This was evidently enough for Little Dick West. He had ridden with real outlaws, and he knew what it was like. It was not like this comic opera. He rode off and never saw his new partners again. He was spotted several months later working on a farm in the area and was killed by marshals while resisting arrest.

In the meantime, the others were poorly dressed, ill equipped, and discouraged. They stuck up Lee Nutter's store at Cushing, Oklahoma, and took new coats, hats, and gloves, the proprietor's watch, fifteen dollars cash money, a jug of whiskey, and a bunch of bananas. The posse that was raised lost their trail in the Creek Nation. They were useless as robbers but they were good at getting away.

Bud Ledbetter had been assigned to another case, and when he brought in that criminal, he and Paden Tolbert were called in to face U.S. Marshal Leo Bennett. The marshal was not happy. The newspapers were full of the stories of the clumsy train robbers who, for all their lack of skill, could not be caught. His instructions were simple, "Go after them and get them, alive if possible—if not, get them anyway."

Deputy marshals Lon Lewis and Joe Thompson in Tulsa heard that the Jennings gang had been spotted on the road to Claremore. When they went to investigate they found a blacksmith north of Tulsa who reported having fixed a horseshoe for one of the gang. He recognized the horse as one he had originally shod for the Spike S ranch belonging to John Harless. Harless, at the time, was in jail awaiting trial on charges of doing some fancy brand "correction" work with a running iron.

The posse gathered on a cold night in November and laid their plans. There were marshals Lewis and Thompson along with Ledbetter and Paden Tolbert. They also had posse members John McClanahan, Gus Thompson, and Jake Elliot. The seven arrived at the Spike S ranch house in the middle of the night and worked out positions for themselves that would cover all approaches to the house. Ledbetter and McClanahan made their way into the barn where they could cover the front.

In order to get a closer look at the house, Ledbetter slipped nearer using a wagon parked in the yard as cover. Morris O'Malley, supposed to be on guard, was sound asleep in the wagon. He awoke with a hand over his mouth and a pistol presenting a strong argument for silence and cooperation. He was soon back in the barn, tied up, gagged, and laid out in a stall.

The first activity from the house was seen just as the sun came up. Clarence Escoe, the brother of Mrs. Harless, came out the door armed with nothing more dangerous than a bucket. He was out for water for the morning coffee and washing. When he realized that O'Malley was nowhere in sight, he went looking and finally went to check the barn. He not only found him, he quickly joined him. He was packaged in the same way and filed away alongside the outlaw.

When the hired girl's announcement that breakfast was ready brought no response from outside, Mrs. Harless came out to hurry along the men. She, too, came to the barn only to discover the law was there in the person of Bud Ledbetter. Rather than add her to his growing collection, Bud told her to go back into the house and tell the gang that they had only two choices, "surrender or die."

When Mrs. Harless went back into the house, her news started a commotion. After some loud discussion and the sounds of furniture being moved around, the two women came back out. Mrs. Harless told Bud: "One of the men wanted to give up, but the red-headed one (that would be Al Jennings) said, 'If the law wants a fight, they can get it,'" and the men started making ready for a battle. The women took shelter behind a stone wall that separated the yard from a small ranch burial ground, and Ledbetter ran to join Paden Tolbert behind the old rock chimney that was all that was left of a burned-out cabin.

Just as he reached the chimney, a shot from the house hit the stone close enough to scatter rock chips in his face. The posse opened fire from all directions, and the shooting became a steady roar. Bullets whipped through the windows and walls. Since most of the shooting was coming from the front of the house, the lawmen worked their way around to that side. When that happened, the outlaws, now all with various wounds, saw a chance to get out a back window and make their escape. They went on foot to the creek and made their way along the bottoms until they were well away from the Spike S.

When Bud learned that they were gone, he reacted strongly. In fact, the posse reported that his comments were "too warm to be recorded." The outlaws' trail died out where they entered the water. After a search the posse finally gave up and returned to Muskogee.

The Jennings brothers and Pat O'Malley took over a wagon being driven by two Native American boys and traveled through the night and holed up the next day. After getting lost trying to make their way to Arkansas without being noticed, they turned the boys loose, kept the wagon, and made their way back to Sam Baker's looking for a place to hide out. After Baker looked at the wounds that Pat O'Malley and Al had received, he insisted that they needed a doctor and that he knew one who would come and not say anything about them.

The wounds were patched up and the three fixed up with a wagon full of straw and directions for getting into Arkansas. They headed out at three o'clock in the morning with Frank driving the team and Al Jennings and O'Malley concealed under the load of straw. The date was December the sixth, and it was bitter cold.

As the wagon started down toward a ford on Carr Creek it had to pass through a cut with high banks on both sides of the road. Just as they were too far into the cut to easily back out they came to a freshly fallen tree lying across the road. There was no room to turn around and, as it turned out, no time to try much of anything.

"Throw away your guns or be killed!" It was Bud Ledbetter's voice. He was concealed in the branches of the downed tree with his rifle sights held on the driver's face. Frank gave up without hesitation. Tolbert and the other two members of the posse announced themselves from the top of the cut on each side of the wagon. Two sets of hands came out of the straw, signaling the surrender of Al Jennings and Pat O'Malley.

Sam Baker had kept his word. While he was in town getting the doctor he had reported to Ledbetter, and the plan to capture the rest of the Jennings gang had been made. The three clumsy outlaws shortly joined Morris O'Malley in the Muskogee jail, and all were eventually sentenced to prison.

Interestingly, there seemed to be no hard feelings on either side. Christmas was only a few weeks away, and shortly after the holiday this note came from the jail for Bud and Paden.

Messrs. Tolbert and Ledbetter,

Dear Sirs and Friends:

Dr. Bennett, USM [Leo Bennett, United States Marshal] and Mr. Lubbes, jailer have kindly delivered to us the excellent Christmas dinner presented by yourselves, which proves you to be connoisseurs as well as men of big hearts and Christmas spirits. We know not if you have any profession of faith, or to what creed you adhere, if any, but we realize that you are Christians at heart.

Therefore, accept our sincere thanks for your generous offer of dinner.

Sincerely,

Pat and Morris O'Malley
Al and Frank Jennings

It is worth recalling that Al and Frank were, after all, lawyers.

The sale of alcoholic beverages was illegal in Indian Territory from its inception, and the work of the law officers, especially the federal deputy marshals, often concerned enforcing the "dry" laws. This was an uncomfortable position for some of them. Their own convictions, like those of many of their fellow citizens, were not opposed to a man having a beer or a drink of whisky once in a while. As a result, the enforcement in particular areas often depended as much on the inclinations of the local officers as it did on the magnitude of the problem.

For Bud Ledbetter it was a clear-cut issue. He had been a teetotaler for most, if not all, of his life. He was convinced that there was no worse influence on a man or a community than strong drink. As a result, few could match his record for sniffing out the shipments of those who would attempt to bring in whiskey. It mattered very little to Bud whether it consisted of a bottle for their own personal use or a wagon load of barrels intended for resale. The operators of "stills" in the hollows and hills of the Northern District of Indian Territory fared no better. Their equipment, supplies, and inventory were the target of Bud's axe just before becoming the fuel for a bonfire.

One of his biggest actions against illegal booze came in October of 1905. Things were pretty much out of hand in Tulsa. The oil boom was on, and liquor and gambling could be found by anyone who wanted it, any time of day. The local officers who would have fought to keep such things under control were themselves pretty much under the thumb of a sheriff who supported, and was possibly supported by, the very elements that were creating the problems.

Two deputy marshals were sent in to get a start on cleaning up the town, but it proved to be more of a job than two men could handle alone. United States Commissioner Samp Jennings ordered a task force led by himself and Bud Ledbetter to plan and carry out a raid on all of the gambling and drinking establishments they could find. After sending in a man undercover to learn the layout of some of the most notorious hangouts, they hit Tulsa on a Friday night in midrevelry. They broke up and burned craps and poker tables, roulette wheels, cards, chips, and dice. The amount of whiskey that was drained out onto the ground from smashed bottles and jugs and broached barrels of various sizes was estimated by the newspaper at "500 to 1000 gallons."

The city marshal, who claimed first that he didn't know there was any gambling going on in Tulsa and then that he "was just getting ready to raid the houses," was soon replaced by one of his officers. That officer had earlier been in trouble with the marshal for making gambling arrests that had not been authorized. The newspaper reported with great satisfaction that it had become difficult to find a place to gamble or to get strong drink of any description.

It was only a week later when that well-known advocate of temperance, Carry A. Nation, arrived in Tulsa. Statehood was being considered for Oklahoma, and the terms and laws that would govern the state were much under discussion. She spoke in Tulsa, displayed her famous hatchet, and announced that she was pleased to learn that she would have no use for it there since Bud Ledbetter "has beaten me to it." Her next stop was in Muskogee, and when she saw Bud in the audience she made a special presentation. She heaped praise on the officer and gave him his own hatchet. She called him "the Carry Nation of Indian Territory." It was not a title he particularly cared for, but it was one he would have a hard time escaping.

"John Cofield's been shot! The killers are barricaded up. Let's go!" Charles Kimsey, chief of police of Muskogee, yanked his buggy to a stop in front of the courthouse and shouted to Bud Ledbetter, who stood on the front steps. Ledbetter grabbed a rifle from inside the courthouse and jumped into the buggy beside the chief. As they pulled away through the muddy street a *Muskogee Phoenix* reporter who happened to be at the courthouse leaped into the back of the buggy and struggled to hang on. Other police officers and deputy marshals Ernest Hubbard and Paul C. Williams scrambled for horses or other transportation to head to the north end of town.

An incident was not completely unexpected. Cofield's assignment had been to serve an eviction notice on a woman named Carrie Foreman. Foreman was a follower of a black preacher named William Wright, who had been the sponsor of more than one venture of dubious repute. This time he was the leader of the Socialist Club and had given the members papers that he claimed gave them the right to occupy any vacant building and stay as long as they wished without paying any rent. Property owners often found this inconvenient and in this case had filed in court to have Foreman removed from the premises.

When Cofield arrived to serve the papers he was met by two armed members of the club, and after a short struggle he was shot through the chest. A man who saw the incident from the street was shot in the arm as he ran to get help. The chief of police received a phone call from Ed Jefferson, a prominent member of the black community in Muskogee, who identified the shooters as Sam and Elbert Barker and warned Kimsey that the men might be wearing armor of some sort.

Because of the chief's warning Bud had passed on his usual rifle, a Winchester chambered for the same .45 round that his Colt pistol fired. He had chosen instead, a new government issued .32 caliber rifle loaded with high-speed steel-jacketed bullets that would pierce any protection the criminals might be wearing.

Bud leaped from the buggy when they were fired on from the two-story house as the police chief was pulling to a stop. The shooting caused the horse to bolt, and the reporter was thrown from the back. He lost no time in finding cover. Kimsey soon got the buggy under control and returned to the scene.

As Ledbetter jumped from the buggy and started toward the building, two men on the porch opened fire, one with a rifle and the other with a pistol. Instantly Bud returned fire, and one of the men flinched as the first bullet hit him. Ledbetter sheltered in the dubious cover of a telephone pole and continued firing with the rifle he had picked up at the courthouse. The man he was shooting at (and hitting) would not go down. About that time Bud was joined at the pole by policeman Paul Smith, who helped him keep up continuous fire. As the first of the men on the porch finally fell and the other stooped to get a better shot at Ledbetter, Bud shot him through the head. Just as he fired that shot, another man took aim at him from a second floor window only to have his arm mangled by a bullet from Paul Smith's weapon. That member of the Socialist Club would survive but lose his right arm.

By this time officers had surrounded the house and the firing was general. It was later determined there were at least nine men in the house involved in the fight. Ledbetter killed two on the front porch. Paul Smith severely wounded the one through the second story window. Two had dragged themselves out of the building to die from their wounds, and four others were arrested. Officers John Cofield and Guy Fisher, both wounded, later recovered. Ledbetter had several bullet holes in his pants but had not received so much as a scratch.

Much was made by some of the press about the "race riot," but race appeared to have had little to do with the affair. From the call made to the chief's office by Mr. Jefferson, to the quick and courageous actions of Paul Smith, a black police officer who probably saved Ledbetter's life, to the statement issued by a large group of Muskogee citizens after the events, everything seems to point to a community consensus rejecting the behavior of the Socialist Club. A group of black citizens met later and declared their support for the actions taken by the officers. Their statement read, in part. ". . . had the members of any race—white, black, red, or brown—shot down an officer in this city in the discharge of his duty and attempted to kill other officials called to the scene, the results would have been the same."

In an interview with the editor of the *Muskogee Phoenix*, Clarence B. Douglass, Bud Ledbetter said, "They shot at me and I just killed them. That's all."

"Were you scared?" the editor asked.

"No, I wasn't scared."

"Were you excited?"

"I wasn't excited none."

"Were you nervous?"

"I'm never nervous."

"Well, you must have had some unusual sensation standing there with them men shooting holes in your britches."

"I don't know about sensation and such." Then Bud added, "I was a little fretted." When the amazed editor pressed for an explanation Ledbetter's answer was, "Well, when I began firing at that porch fellow with that fancy little government rifle, I knowed I was hitting him in the belly every shot, and when he wouldn't fall it fretted me. Tell you somethin', Colonel—never go after a shooting man with one of them newfangled .32s. Get you hurt if you do. Always take a .45—that knocks 'em down and they don't get up and bother you no more."

The newspaper reported later that Sam Barker had received several wounds close together in the center of the abdomen made by small caliber bullets that passed completely through the body without expanding. He probably would have died from any of them, but there was little or no shock of impact that would have taken him immediately out of the fight.

After statehood in 1907 the role of the federal marshal's office was much reduced, and most of the officers went on to other work. Ledbetter became the only officer in the small town of Webbers Falls for a couple of months. Then he had the more exciting offer of becoming the town marshal for Haskell,

Bud Ledbetter
(photo courtesy of University of Oklahoma Libraries)

which had become a pretty wild oil boomtown. It did not take long to settle Haskell down, and when the city of Muskogee needed a chief of police he was again ready for a change.

The move back to Muskogee was not a happy one for the Ledbetters. Bud was enmeshed in a political struggle from the very beginning. The job was an elected position, and there was much opposition from the businesses of the sort that might expect to have trouble with an honest officer determined to enforce the laws against alcoholic beverages. Bud won the election but shortly after lost the job because of a lawsuit that challenged the city's status under the new state constitution. When he was asked to serve out an unexpired term as sheriff of Muskogee County in 1912 he accepted. When the time came, he ran and was elected to the office on his own.

By the end of that second term Bud was in his middle sixties and decided to slow down and farm. He did that and also assisted in the filming of the movie *The Passing of the Oklahoma Outlaws* in 1915. He directed the scenes of the Spike S fight and played himself as that part of the movie was filmed on location at the ranch. He might not have gotten involved if he had not seen the depiction of himself and other territorial officers in the film *Beating Back* made by Al Jennings. Jennings had been pardoned and was touring the country showing his movie and lecturing on the evils of living a life of crime. The movie, however, made that life look pretty glamorous and showed the officers of the law as venal and basically incompetent.

In protest, *The Passing of the Oklahoma Outlaws* was made by former U.S. Marshal E. D. Nix and former deputies Chris Madsen and Bill Tilghman to try to put the story straight. Bud was heard to comment that he should have shot Jennings somewhere besides the leg.

Bud was talked into coming off the farm in 1917 to clean up another boomtown. This time it was Okmulgee, Oklahoma, where he served as the force's only plain clothes vice detective until 1922 when he returned to the farm. It didn't last but a few months.

The next year Bud, nearing seventy, reluctantly let himself be talked into accepting the nomination of the Democratic Party to run for sheriff of Muskogee County once again. In spite of his own expressed doubts, he won easily and served two terms, finally retiring at last in 1928.

The man who had never been so much as wounded through years of confrontations with outlaws and uncounted gunfights, who steadfastly refused to talk or brag about his exploits, died quietly in his bed of heart disease in 1936. His children were at his side, and he was held high in the thoughts of those who knew the contribution he had made to law and order in Arkansas, Indian Territory, and Oklahoma.

The eulogy delivered at Bud's funeral by his friend State Senator Gid Graham ended with these words: "I am proud to have known this man whose three traits of character were kindness, courage, and rugged honesty."

Chris Madsen

Soldier/Lawman

Even the most prosaic recitation of Christian Madsen's background makes interesting history. He was born in 1851 in Denmark. His father was a military man, and Chris learned early what was expected of a soldier. He was fourteen when he first became one. He served with the Danish army against the invading Germans. When he was forced out of Denmark by his country's defeat, he made his way to Algeria where he served in the French Foreign Legion. His Legion was returned to Europe during the Franco-Prussian War, and Chris was wounded, then taken prisoner at the battle of Sedan. When he was well enough, he broke out of the prisoner of war camp and joined a band of French partisans, who continued to harass the Germans for the rest of the conflict.

When the war ended, Chris followed his dream. He had saved all he could to make his passage to America possible. He wanted to fight Indians. He had read the glamorous descriptions of the Indian fighters, and he wanted to be one. There he thought he could make a mark fighting against savagery and for civilization.

He had no trouble enlisting when he arrived in New York in 1876. He found a recruiting station and signed up as a member of the Seventh Cavalry. During the physical examination, the doctor asked something like, "How did you get that scar on your ankle?"

The answer was, ". . . the battle of Sedan in France."

The doctor asked a few questions to satisfy himself that this little foreigner with the unusual accent wasn't ribbing him. In the process he got the rest of the story. When the doctor understood all he was being told, he announced that he thought the U.S. Army could find a place for Chris fighting Indians.

His background, combat experience, and the fact that he would need no basic training brought quick responsibility and a change of assignment. He was one of a hundred men transferred to the Fifth Cavalry to fill its ranks. If not for that change, Chris might have found himself with Custer at the Little Big Horn instead of being assigned to the burial detail there a few days later.

From his enlistment in 1876 through 1880 he participated in campaigns against the Sioux and Cheyenne, the Nez Perce, the Bannocks, twice against the Cheyenne, and finally, the Utes. There was also a later hard ride from Kansas into Indian Territory to put down a bloody uprising of the Cheyenne and Arapaho there. The Army conducted an intense search and collected many second-hand stories of atrocities but found no one who had actually seen any of them. The "bloodthirsty savages" were finally located, on their reservation, minding their own business. They were surprised to learn that they had supposedly been on the warpath.

In 1885 he was returned with his unit to Fort Riley, Kansas. The announcement had been officially made. The Indian Wars were over. There would be no more trouble. That, of course, would pass like so many rumors of peace since time forgotten, but for a while things were quiet.

Soon Chris was promoted to sergeant and detailed to be quartermaster of the troop. This led to a problem involving civilian suppliers that eventually caused him to face a court-martial accused of mishandling government money. He was quickly acquitted, but related charges were then brought in a civilian court. This time Chris was convicted and sentenced to several months in prison. He served his time, but it is questionable if he had committed any grave dereliction of duty. As soon as he was released from prison the army not only reinstated him with full rank and pay, he was once again assigned as quartermaster and given the same duties as before. General Nelson Miles called on Madsen repeatedly and sent him to one post or another to get the supply records and accounts in order.

Men are often called on in military service to use whatever abilities and experiences life has given them. Unfortunately, it did not occur to Chris to say "no" when the post commander at Fort Riley asked if he knew how to dance. Well, perhaps not so unfortunate after all. It was a difficult assignment and not one to be relished by a soldier but, "for the morale of the troops," he became the post dancing instructor. The commandant's idea was that if they learned to dance and the fort sponsored dances, it would be a genteel entertainment and everyone would be happy.

It was a campaign much like any other. First Chris trained the troops, then he scouted out the enemy. Word was sent out to all the surrounding towns and farms that free dancing lessons were available at the fort for any young ladies who wished to take advantage of them. Free entertainment on the Kansas plains! The girls flocked to the fort and Chris went on teaching. At one lesson Chris demonstrated a step with the help of a young lady named Maggie Morris. After he held her and looked into her eyes, teaching dancing was not such a burden for a soldier anymore. Her father was less impressed with the idea but was eventually won over.

Soon Chris was transferred to Fort Reno, Indian Territory. However, love was helped by one of those coincidences that shouldn't but do occur in the lives of men. The Morris family moved to a farm not far from Fort Reno. The friendship between Chris and Maggie was renewed, and in December of 1887 they were married.

In 1891 Madsen chose not to reenlist. He had been disillusioned with the idea of fighting Indians for some time. The right and wrong were not as clear as he had imagined them to be while he was still in Europe. The "savages" turned out to be pretty normal people whose reactions to the events affecting them he could understand. Their numbers included the wise and the stupid, the generous and the mean, the excitable and the calm. In fact, they were very much like every other group of people that Chris had dealt with in his travels. He was also very aware of the fact that treaty after treaty had been broken by the U.S. government. Now the problem was what would he do? He wanted something where he could use his skills but know for sure that he was on the "right" side.

The answer arrived just before his enlistment was up. A visitor asked for him at Fort Reno. William Grimes was the newly appointed United States marshal for Oklahoma Territory. He was trying to recruit deputies and having no small amount of trouble finding the right kind of men. He needed officers with the skills and the willingness to go up against the outlaws that had come to see the Territories as great places to hide out from the law. He had approached officers at the fort for ideas. Someone thought of Sergeant Madsen, who had already made it clear that he was going to give civilian life a try. Chris was surprised. What did he know about law enforcement? He was a soldier. Grimes urged him to think about it.

At that time Chris was making top money for an army sergeant, twenty-nine dollars a month. After agreeing to talk to "his Maggie" about it, he asked, almost as an afterthought, about the pay. Grimes told him that deputies would earn two hundred and fifty dollars a month. Chris asked him to repeat the figure and then decided perhaps talking to Maggie would not be necessary after all.

So, he left the Army and accepted a commission as deputy United States marshal to be stationed at El Reno, Oklahoma Territory. He served there and later at Guthrie, the territorial capital. It was not long before the recruitment of deputies brought into his life two of the best friends and working partners he would ever have.

Heck Thomas reported for duty in Guthrie and explained that he was being transferred from the jurisdiction of the court of the Western District of Arkansas. He had an outstanding record in the Indian Territory serving Judge Parker's court. They would work together for many years.

Bill Tilghman was next; he had worked in Dodge with the Earps and the Mastersons but was known as a straight arrow, a man who served the community first. He did not hang around in saloons, didn't supplement his income as a gambler, and did not allow politics to influence his enforcement of the law. These three not only became fast friends, their names became so linked with the effort to bring order and peace to the wild territories that they were known as The Three Guardsmen of Oklahoma.

In an early bit of action, Chris, Heck Thomas, and Tom Hueston went to a farm near the town of Orlando. The place belonged to the sister of bank robber Ol Yantis. They set up watch during the night and were rewarded just as the sun came up. Ol came out of the house with a pistol in one hand and a sack of feed in the other. Madsen identified the trio as officers and ordered Yantis to raise his hands. Yantis raised his six-gun instead and got off one shot before Chris put a bullet in him. Ol staggered but didn't go down and was able to fire another shot before Hueston fired and the outlaw dropped. Yantis was taken to town for medical care but died during the night.

Chris Madsen was a short, square-built man and tended toward the pudgy. This sometimes got him underestimated by opponents, especially if they were too drunk to take in his military bearing and the air of confidence with which he acted.

He made a trip with Judge Burford and a traveling court consisting of all the necessary equipment and three wagon loads of prisoners to Beaver City in the far western reaches of the Territory. It was necessary because the men had to be tried in the area where the crimes they were accused of were committed. They had all been relocated to towns like Guthrie, El Reno, and Dodge City, Kansas, because there were no secure jails in "No Man's Land."

The residents of the Panhandle were used to being pretty much left alone by the authorities. They certainly were not all criminals, but they did share a preference for taking care of their own business that included not being bothered by the federal courts and officers. As a result, the officers of the court received several warnings on the way out that the reception waiting for them in Beaver City was not likely to be cordial. The warnings were accurate but did not sway the judge or the marshals who accompanied him.

Not only was the jail full so that the prisoners being brought in had to continue to sleep on the ground while chained to the wagon wheels, but there were no accommodations for the court. Chris and the district judge were trying to get a night's sleep in the room that had been set up as a courtroom. It was over a saloon but the only place that was available. The noise from below was bad, but they had to consider it unavoidable if they wanted a place to sleep indoors. Then the celebration got out of hand. When the festivities progressed to the point that the fellows were firing off their pistols into the ceiling, something had to be done. The bullets, of course, came right up through the floor of the room occupied by the judge and the deputy marshal.

Chris went downstairs quickly to settle things down before someone got hurt. The first floor was divided into two rooms: The larger at the front was for gambling and the other, through a narrow pair of swinging doors, was the barroom. When Chris got downstairs nothing was going on in the gambling room, but that was where the shooting had to have been done. He stepped to the swinging doors in time to hear a somewhat intoxicated cowboy suggest to his two friends that they go back in the other room and shoot some more "fly-specks" off the ceiling.

The first man stepped through the swinging doors and was met by Chris. The deputy marshal grabbed the cowboy's pistol and twisted it out of his hand. That action was resented by the next man through the doors, who announced loudly, "I'm a son-of-a-bitch from Cripple Creek." Madsen's response, which would have come in that slight Danish accent he never lost, is supposed to have been, "I knew who you were, but I didn't know where you were from." That brought a punch thrown at the deputy. It didn't connect because Chris "buffaloed" the man with the pistol he was holding. The third of the happy celebrants decided to express his displeasure, but when he went for his six-gun Chris shot him in the gun arm. He arrested all three men and locked them up. There were no more incidents to disrupt the judge's sleep.

That night Chris was warned again that he better get out of town because the cowboys who worked with the three he had arrested would be coming for him. He simply answered that he would be there if they were looking for him. It didn't take long. Two men with the look more of gunfighters than of cowboys rode in later. Chris met them on the street as they stepped down from their mounts. When he asked if he could do something for them, the answer was they had come to see the new deputy marshal.

Chris told them they had seen him now and they could climb back on their horses and go. When they hesitated, he said, ". . . do you go now, or do I have to kill you?" They had planned to do the "running out of town." This was not the way it was supposed to go. They did not have the will to resist Madsen, so they went, and when he ordered them to hurry, they hurried.

Beaver City in the Panhandle, or "No Man's Land" as it was often called, was not the longest trip Chris Madsen ever made to bring back a prisoner. He was sent to Fort Sill in the southwest part of the Territory in response to a telegram to the marshal's office asking for assistance. When he got there he was told that a soldier named Peter Schneider was wanted.

He had been a very popular trooper and a good soldier. He played his accordion for the dances on the base or anytime that music was called for. Some soldiers from the fort showed up at a civilian dance in Medicine Creek where he had been invited to play. One of the soldiers had enjoyed the party a little too much and was, as the saying goes, "feeling no pain." When Schneider tried to reason with him and even stopped the music and put the accordion down, the soldier refused to listen. In the midst of the argument the soldier completely lost his temper and took a vigorous kick at the accordion. It was ruined. Schneider picked up the remains of his instrument and headed back to the fort. Evidently he was building up a head of steam all the way.

When he got to the fort he armed himself with a butcher knife from the kitchen and headed partway back along the trail to Medicine Creek. When his drunken antagonist came along in the dark, Peter Schneider acted and then disappeared. He was no longer a model soldier.

Chris was given the task of finding Schneider and bringing him in. The trail eventually led from the Territory to Texas and then to California. In Los Angeles he found that the soldier had gone north. After much searching, Madsen was back on the track when he found a ranch near San Francisco where Schneider had worked, but he was too late again. He had been gone for a few days and had told an acquaintance that he was saving up his money to buy passage to Australia.

When Chris got back to San Francisco it seemed that his quarry had already left the country. He could not be sure so he determined to watch the waterfront for a few days. He asked a policeman for help in finding a place to stay and explained his mission. The officer asked for a description of the wanted man, and when Chris had given it he said, "There he goes now!" and pointed at a ship maneuvering to leave the harbor. He explained that a man just like Chris described had asked him for directions to the ship. It was sailing for Australia.

Chris had chased him for so long and had come that close to catching him. As he fretted about the situation, a boat belonging to the United States Army came into dock. Chris recognized one of the officers who was leaving the ship as a man, now a captain, he had served with in the Fifth Cavalry.

He laid out the situation to the captain who relayed it to the general in charge, and the army craft was soon signaling the liner to hold up. Then Chris was taken alongside the ship, and the uniformed officers explained what was needed to the ship's captain, and Chris soon had the handcuffs on his man. After a few days for jurisdictional paperwork, the two men were on their way back to Oklahoma but this time together. Schneider was sentenced to life in prison for murder.

George "Red Buck" Weightman was one of the worst outlaws and killers ever seen in Texas and Oklahoma. It is pretty rare that a bad man gets kicked out of an outlaw gang because he is too vicious and cold-blooded. Weightman had a long record as a horse thief and murderer. He was captured in 1889 by Heck Thomas and served a term in prison for stealing horses. When he got out he joined the Doolin gang and was involved in the big shootout when they were surrounded at Ingalls, but he managed to get away.

He stayed with the gang another year and a half until they were fleeing from a successful train robbery during which Red Buck's horse had been killed. They stopped at the farm of an elderly preacher, and Weightman took a horse from the corral. When the old man wobbled out of the cabin and objected, the outlaw shot him dead even though he was unarmed and could not have done anything about the theft.

The gang made good their escape, but when they had reached safety, Doolin and Bill Dalton had a quick talk, and Doolin tossed a share of the loot to Weightman and told him to light out on his own. They wanted nothing more to do with him. Doolin was smart enough to know that killings like that of the old minister were not only unnecessary, they just caused trouble for the outlaws. Actions like that took away any sympathy they might be able to generate in the country-side and made the law even more determined to catch them. Things were already bad enough since Dalton had killed a law officer in a previous robbery and that always heated up the pursuit.

This rejection apparently didn't faze Red Buck. He got some other hard cases together and organized his own gang and continued his depredations on a wide swath of the coun-tryside. After being wounded in a hard fight with Texas Rangers in north Texas, Weightman returned to the Oklahoma Territory. He went to ground, literally, in a dugout in the west-ern part of the territory near Cheyenne.

When word came to Madsen he organized a posse and went after the Weightman gang. The posse surrounded the dugout, and Chris ordered Red Buck to come out and give up. The bad man tried to shoot his way out once again, but this time it didn't work. When he tried to get out of the cabin door, Madsen shot and killed him.

It was during 1895 that the worn old wagon pulled up in front of the Madsen home in El Reno. Anna, wife of Whirl-wind, a Cheyenne chief, came up the walk followed by a string of children of various ages. Chris welcomed them into his home but was curious about the reason for the visit and won-dered about Whirlwind himself. Where was he?

Anna took a Cheyenne pipe from her blanket and handed it to Chris. She told him, in effect, that the old chief was dead and that he, Madsen, was now head of their family. It was the way Whirlwind had said it would be if anything ever happened to him. They were happy to be there, and now they knew everything would be all right.

While Chris was still quartermaster sergeant at Fort Reno, one of the jobs that fell to him was the issuing of supplies to the Cheyenne whose reservation adjoined the fort. That made him a very important man in their eyes. He was also a fair and honest man, and those he dealt with knew it. He and Whirlwind— Chris always called him "Chief Whirlwind"— became particularly close.

They talked about many things, but one subject was taboo. Whirlwind had fought at the Little Big Horn against Custer and never wanted that subject to come up with whites. It had never occurred to Chris that they had become so close that Whirlwind would leave him his family.

They moved right in. This was where their father had told them they must go, and they were happy to be here. Chris and Maggie were too stunned to object and did not want to hurt the feelings of their newly bereaved guests, but what were they going to do with a house full of people who expected to stay permanently? They managed for a few days. Anna tried to help with the cooking. The children tried not to make too much noise when they got up at dawn. Anna chopped a bunch of weeds out of the garden. Chris didn't try to explain that it was the parsley.

Finally, they could take no more, and they made Anna understand that she needed to take the children and go back to the reservation. It would have been hard to tell who felt worse, the Cheyenne children who were leaving their fascinating new home or Maggie and Chris.

Chris Madsen
(photo courtesy of Univeristy of Oklahoma Libraries)

The reputations of Madsen, Tilghman, and Thomas grew
to such an extent that sometimes their names alone were
enough to work magic on the tough guys of the Territory. Chris
and Heck Thomas were on the trail of the leader of a gang of
horse rustlers named Three-Finger Roberts in the vicinity of
Rush Springs. They didn't know Roberts by sight so they arranged with the local blacksmith to have his young son point
out the outlaw on the street. When the boy did, he indicated a
group of toughs standing together in front of a hotel. Chris and
Heck ordered the men to put up their hands. No one moved.
The two officers had moved in close and were outnumbered.
Even though they had their weapons in their hands, there was
no certainty that they could kill all of the men who faced them
if it came to a gunfight.

The officers and the bad men continued to stare each
other down and stand ready for a fight until a bystander
declared, "It's Chris Madsen and Heck Thomas." Toughness
seemed to evaporate as hands moved carefully away from pistols and started for the sky.

They ordered Roberts to drop his gunbelt and step for-
ward. The cuffs went on the horse thief, and he was loaded
into the wagon. The others scattered as soon as they had permission, and the deputies headed back to close out the case.

Maggie Morris Madsen was a well-liked neighbor and a
much-loved spouse, but Maggie was never blessed with good
health. In 1897 she was diagnosed with what was then called
"consumption." Chris had been transferred to the marshal's office in Kansas City, and the colder climate was not helping. He
brought her back to their house in El Reno with the children
but did not feel he could give up his job, and so he returned to

Kansas City. In March it was obvious she was not getting better so he resigned and came home.

Maggie could have anything she wanted—always could as far as he was concerned. Now she wanted to go back to their farm. It reminded her of her happy childhood. They moved to the farm, and when her health declined Chris insisted on the doctor coming out to the farm every day. It was expensive, but he mortgaged the farm to pay for it. Nothing was too good for "his Maggie." As was commonly the case in those days, with that diagnosis, the end was inevitable. Maggie died at their farm in May of 1898.

Now he faced a handful of problems. His daughter was nine, his son eight. He had no job, no money left, and a mortgage hanging over his head. As it always seemed to do for him, something, "turned up." This time it was a telegram. Colonel Leonard Wood, United States Army, wanted Christian Madsen to come immediately to San Antonio, Texas, and take over the job of quartermaster sergeant for the Rough Riders. The recruitment was on for the attack on Cuba. But Chris could not go; he answered and declined because of the children.

The next wire begged him to reconsider, offered suggestions for what to do about his son and daughter, and urged him to come because his help was needed. After much agonizing he finally agreed to leave little Marion Morris Madsen and Christian Madsen Jr., known always as "Reno," in the care of neighbors and hurry to Texas to join the Teddy Roosevelt's Rough Riders.

As in the case of so many who went to Cuba, the effects of the "fever" were worse than any combat. Chris never saw a shot fired in the four months he was away. He was given a medical discharge and came home eighty pounds lighter than he left. It took three months in bed to recover. He spent them at the farm with neighbors looking after him. When he had improved some he moved into town and stayed with friends until he could get along on his own.

Near the end of the year he had improved enough that he wrote to the United States marshal in Ardmore and inquired about the possibility of returning to the federal service. It only took a few days for the answer to come back. A telegram from the attorney general's office in Washington D.C. instructed him to report to Marshal John Hammer at Ardmore. He packed his guns and caught the train. He was back in harness again.

Some things never change. One constant in the life of a deputy U.S. marshal was the payment of his expense account or rather, the nonpayment of that account. A deputy would be out a lot of money making a sweep and bringing in a group of prisoners. They had to be fed along the way. Horses had to be cared for, sometimes a wagon repaired or a doctor paid for services to an officer or a prisoner. It added up, and Washington never seemed to be in a hurry to get the expense checks to the field to reimburse the men.

Chris and Bill Tilghman determined to go to the nation's capital and see if they could influence the procedures that kept officers from getting paid their expense money in a timely manner. Some of the unpaid accounts had been submitted for over a year and were still in the same condition. It was early in 1909 and President, once Colonel, Teddy Roosevelt was holding one last big social affair before his term in office was completed. When he was told that Chris Madsen was in the capital, nothing would do but Chris must have a special invitation to the swan song soiree.

It didn't seem possible that a couple of middle-aged, horseback outlaw chasers could manage themselves at such an event. With serious misgivings they found a place to rent formal wear suitable for the occasion and made their appearance. Their discomfort showed like a busted lip on a socialite. As they tried their best to fit in, Tilghman saw a British diplomat nod toward them and speak to the lady he was escorting. "Look at those crude Americans," he said, "what a country to produce such men."

That did not set too well with Bill. He looked around until he found someone he knew and brought him over to meet Chris. "I want you to meet the new ambassador from Denmark—Christian Madsen, who has just arrived in our country." Chris fell into the game immediately. When the diplomat heard that accent he bought the story. Tilghman and Madsen played it to the hilt with Bill even calling Chris, "Your Highness." The evening no longer seemed so intimidating. They had scalded the cat, and nothing was going to scare them out of having a good time now.

Chris took some time off from law enforcement in 1916 to join with Tilghman and E. D. Nix, the former U.S. marshal for Indian Territory, to make a movie. *The Passing of the Oklahoma Outlaws* was intended to be the law officer's answer to one called *Beating Back*, by Al Jennings. Jenning's film, ostensibly made to accompany his lectures on the evils of a life of crime, still managed to show the men who enforced the law in a bad light. He made them appear corrupt and trigger-happy. The film, unlike Al's accompanying lecture, seemed to glorify the outlaw life. All of the old-time law officers who saw *Beating Back* were offended, and many of them

111

were willing to help get their version of the "old days" on film for people to see. Madsen served as secretary to their production company and played himself in the movie. He briefly toured with the movie. He made lectures and tried to give the world a vision of the truth as seen from behind a badge.

Chris returned to law enforcement in 1918 as special investigator for the governor's office until 1922 when he retired and spent the next twenty years writing about his life. He worked on a manuscript that he intended to be his autobiography and had a number of articles about his life published in the local papers. He loved to spend his time hanging around the sheriff's office and the police station talking about the old days.

As he aged, he lost his old friends. Illness claimed Heck Thomas in 1912, and Bill Tilghman returned to harness at the governor's request in 1924. Chris advised him not to go, but Bill agreed to try to put a lid on the oil boomtown of Cromwell, Oklahoma. He was shot to death in October of that year by Wylie Linn, a federal prohibition agent who was intoxicated at the time of the shooting.

In 1927 his son, Reno, gave him a trip he had been talking about for a long time. They took a car trip west to revisit the battlefield at the Little Big Horn. As they drove along an empty stretch of Wyoming road they found a car stranded. The driver explained that he needed the use of an air pump to inflate a flat tire. Reno got his out, and the man started to repair his flat. As he worked he explained that he was Cheyenne and was taking his father somewhere. In the casual conversation, and as a matter of ancient history, the man mentioned that his father had fought at the Battle of the Little Big Horn. Chris heard that and decided it would be interesting to compare notes with the other old veteran of those long past wars. He got out and went to the other car and tried to talk to him, but even after half a century, the fear of reprisal was too great. The old Cheyenne pretended to speak no English and got out of the car and started walking down the road. He kept right on going until the son had the car fixed and caught up with him. He got back in the car, and they were gone.

Chris had met several of the men from the other side of that battle but had never been able to get any of them to talk to him about it. They never found out how sympathetic Chris was to their side of the overall dispute that led to that battle, one of the few that Native-Americans could claim as complete victories. Of course, that victory did not sustain the Indian Nations for very long. They were too badly outnumbered.

Chris looked around the battlefield and had difficulty locating things. The years and the building of various monuments had changed the appearance of the land so much that he had to guess about the locations of some of the action. Finally they came to the impressive monument which memorialized all those who had died. As he went through the list of names, he came to one that was a shock. It was in the "M"s, Madsen, Christian. He was shocked. It felt like a deception on his part to let his name be listed among those dead on that battlefield. His appeals to the management of the park and to the administrators in Washington did no good. Christian Madsen was listed as dead in combat with hostiles and that's the way it would have to stay. Chris was upset and would hardly speak of it again. It now seems that there was a man by that name killed that day and that the name on the monument was a matter of coincidence rather than confusion.

He spent his life urging respect for the law. Even in old age it was a favorite topic of conversation as he made his way around Guthrie keeping up with those few of his old friends who were left. As age grew on him, his memories stretched themselves further into his past and he spoke of Denmark, fighting the Germans, both there and in the French Foreign Legion. He sometimes said he had fought in four wars and always won, "but maybe I don't this time." Chris Madsen died in the Masonic Home for the Aged in 1944. He would have soon been ninety-three years old. He had been one of the "good guys" for a long time.

Jeff Milton
Seventy Years of Doing
What He Knew Was Right

"When I die, I hope they have something better to say about me than to tell how many men I've killed." Jeff Milton, in his eighties, was listening to his wife read the obituary of one of his old friends, another man who had lived by his guns but survived to old age. Jeff did not like to talk much about the men he had killed, but he would tell people about the ones he "ought to have killed" but didn't. The ones who wouldn't fight when he faced them. "You just can't hardly kill a man like that." He preferred to talk about the horses that had been his partners in work for most of his life or the friends who had stood by him in one trouble or another.

Jefferson Davis Milton was born in November of 1861 while his father was the governor of Florida, Confederate States of America. Jeff longed for adventure and found it. At sixteen he had worked on ranches in deep southwest Texas and had a reputation both as a good man in a fight and a good man on the trail. By eighteen, he was hard, lean, a good judge and caretaker of horses, and as good as you can get with a .45 single action Colt or a long gun of any sort.

He wanted to prove himself with the fighting men he most admired, so he grew a mustache, claimed an additional three years of age, and joined the Texas Rangers. He served all over

Texas, from the Indian fights in the northwest plains to the border disputes on the Rio Grande. During this time he met many of the men who were to play parts in his later life—some good, some bad, and some who managed to change from one category to the other while he knew them.

There was enough action in the Rangers to suit even him. He was with a detachment of Company B when it was sent to calm the new railroad town of Colorado City in 1881. One of the instant tent cities that sprang up at each section location on the railroad, it was set up to support the railroad's construction. These attracted the worst sorts of camp followers seeking to lighten the wallets of the railroad workers while furnishing their needs and their wants. In that part of the state they were also frequently the closest place for cowboys working that range to find a drink, some food, and some fun.

The Rangers' first order in Colorado City was to ban carrying weapons in town. They were occasionally forced to remove a cowboy's guns against his will, but for the most part it worked and things became much quieter. In spite of this, one day as Jeff and a Ranger named Williams were passing John Birdwell's saloon, a man came to tell them there was someone at the bar and "couldn't no Ranger take his pistol off of him." Another man came out of the saloon and told them that anyone who tried to get that man's gun was going to get killed. Jeff and Williams looked at each other and Jeff said, "If we don't get that six-shooter, we might as well quit the service."

In the saloon they saw a man whose coat showed the outline of what was obviously a pistol. He stood with his back to them and kept up a roar on the subject of how he would just like to see the man who could take a gun away from him. Jeff drew his Colt, stuck it in the man's back, and said, "I'll take it."

When he relieved the man's pocket of a sawed-off piece of plow handle the tent shook with laughter. Jeff laughed like the rest, then bought a round for everyone. The Ranger who played so many practical jokes on others could take one on himself. He also added to his reputation for dealing with situations without fear.

Jeff Milton served in the Texas Rangers for three years, longer than most, but he had enjoyed the company and found the adventure he wanted. By May of 1883 many of the best of the great old Rangers that he served under had gone back to more prosaic pursuits or had left to become law officers in local jurisdictions of one sort or another. It wasn't as much fun as it had been so he resigned and took the first job he came across, as a dry-goods clerk for Dan Murphy in Fort Davis, Texas. That embarrassed his rowdy friends, but Jeff was always one to take whatever work came to hand.

Working in a store didn't last very long. An old friend from the Rangers, Charlie Neville, by then the sheriff, deputized him and sent him to keep the peace at a railroad town and cowboy watering place called Murphyville, which had started as a switch point on a ranch belonging to Jeff's boss at the store. It was the first settlement in the area that eventually became Alpine, Texas.

Since most of the problems of the growing town came from rambunctious cowboys enjoying themselves, creating peace was mostly a matter of gathering up the ones who had overdone things and letting them sober up. There was no jail so Jeff locked them up in an old boxcar on a railroad siding. One morning when he got up his jail was gone and some prisoners with it. Some frantic telegraphy by the Southern Pacific agent, up and down the line, located the car. A train had picked it up during the night, and Jeff had to go recover his charges.

It didn't take much enforcement to have a calming effect on the town, and the cowboys mostly were good natured. However, good nature and regard for the representative of law and order in Murphyville did not eliminate the need to have a good time. Soon some of the boys found great fun in going out to one edge of the community and firing off a few shots, which would invariably bring Jeff at a hard run. As soon as they had loosed a volley they circled around the few buildings that made up the town to come up on the other end and shoot some more, again bringing the law running, as hard as he could, back the other way.

That game came to an end one night after Milton loaded a couple of shotgun shells with the lightest shot he could find, number ten, and arranged for a friend to help him. When the shooting started, the friend took off at a run toward the noise, and Jeff went to the other end of town and hid in the tall grass. When they came to his end of town, laughing at the joke they were playing on the deputy, the deputy was ready. As they cut loose so did Jeff, and the blast of the shotgun in the dark and the sting of the birdshot put an abrupt end to their play.

After things settled down in Murphyville Jeff tried his hand in the saloon business. He sold out after two hours when he decided that, while he didn't have anything against drinking and didn't mind going on a "little toot" once in a while himself, he didn't have the patience to put up with drunks on a regular basis. So, for a while, he did a little hunting, took on jobs for Sheriff Neville, which afforded him the opportunity for some shooting and fighting for reasons his integrity could live with, and just generally enjoyed life. Restless, he eventually started west again and found country to his liking in Socorro County in western New Mexico. He cowboyed, managed a ranch, homesteaded a place for himself, and eventually became a deputy under Sheriff Charlie Russell, another ex-Ranger. Nothing held him for very long, and he finally took a contract to form a crew, gather a herd, and deliver it for sale for one of the biggest ranchers in the area, Kim Ki Rogers.

On this drive, while they were camped north of Elephant Butte near the holding of an elderly Mexican man who had a half dozen head of stock on the range, Jeff sent a rider to kill a beef for the cook. When he got back in at the end of the day the meat was hanging on the wagon spokes, but the hide was nowhere in sight. The practice was to hang your hides up in plain view so that anyone could see from the brand that you were eating your own beef. When he asked the cook about it and was told that the man threw the hide in the river, Jeff wanted to know why.

"He didn't want anyone to find it," was the answer. "He killed a beef belonging to that old Mexican that he don't like."

"Hell he did," was Jeff's angry response.

When Milton told the story in later years, he remembered that he made the cowboy drag the river until he found the hide, stretch it, then go pay the owner for the beef. Then he fired him.

After Jeff came back from a trip home to Florida financed by the money made on the drive, he received an invitation to become a deputy from the sheriff in St. Johns, Arizona, a man with the unlikely name of Commodore Perry Owens. A friend from New Mexico who had moved farther west while Milton was visiting home had recommended him. He went and within a week found out that he and Owens were not going to "hit it off together." Jeff left for El Paso where another friend had arranged an interview for him with Joseph Magoffin, collector of customs. The job was to watch the entire border of Arizona and Mexico for contraband goods. In Tucson, he reported to W. S. Oury, an old-time fighting man, born in Virginia and raised in Texas. Oury welcomed the young Milton because of his Southern and Texan pedigree and showed him the ropes of his new job.

Jeff Milton
(photo courtesy of University of Oklahoma Libraries)

Riding the border looking for smugglers was just the life for Jeff, and it was there that he formed a lasting friendship with one of the most unusual characters of the border. During a time of close cooperation between the two countries, Jeff was assigned to work with the dynamic commander of the Mexican federal troops who guarded that stretch of desert, Colonel Emilio Kosterlitzky. Their joint purpose was to find and stop a bandit gang led by "Black Jack" Ketchum, which was operating on both sides of the border. They met at San Bernardino, the ranch of another hard man with a long history of being willing and able to enforce what he saw as right, John Slaughter, ex-Texas Ranger and soon to be sheriff of Cochise County.

While mutual respect was apparent from the beginning, the real personal friendship between the Russian-born Mexican officer and Jeff began on one of their trips together into the Sierra Madre looking for Ketchum and his men. As they carefully approached a remote cabin, a man ran out and took cover behind a tree. When he exposed himself just enough to take aim at Kosterlitzky, Jeff killed him with one quick shot from the saddle. The two men were fast friends from then on and worked together frequently while Milton served as a federal agent along that border.

Trouble does not take long to find you when you become chief of police of a tough town with a reputation for being hard on its law officers. Jeff Milton may have been expecting that when he accepted the post of chief of police in El Paso, Texas, in August of 1894; but expecting it or not, it was there. "Uncle John" Selman, a notorious gunman, who may have had as many as twenty notches on his gun before coming to El Paso, had been serving as constable of one precinct for two years. He and his deputies were doing quite well on the protection money that they demanded from the "working girls" of the "Tenderloin," El Paso's red-light district.

Selman had some things to say around town about just what he intended to do about this upstart new police chief. They mostly involved some creative uses for Chief Milton's gun after he had taken it away from him. Word of Selman's talk came to Milton on his first day in office, and the chief promptly found his detractor holding forth at the bar of a saloon. Selman did not know Milton was there until he felt a hand on his shoulder and heard the soft greeting, "Hello, Uncle John." Jeff mentioned that he was wearing his six-shooter and asked if Selman still wanted to use it on him. He didn't. That was not the end of problems with him, but it certainly stopped it for that day. It is interesting to note that among the officers Milton selected for his reorganized police force was "Young John" Selman of whom the chief said, "he was the best boy to have the sorriest daddy" he had ever seen.

The new chief's next action was to get a list of all the shady to downright crooked gamblers in town by the simple expedient of paying one of them a hundred dollars out of his own pocket. He alphabetized the names and called on the first ten. He told them to be on the next train out of town or they would be arrested. He gave that warning to the next ten the next day. The *El Paso Times* reported that there was a good deal of immigration from El Paso into Lordsburg, New Mexico, following the first week of this policy and that the folks of Lordsburg did not seem all that grateful. Most of the tinhorns got the idea after the first couple of days and looked for greener pastures without waiting for a personal invitation.

Another old friend who was frequently involved in Jeff's exploits was George Scarborough. They had known each other since their days as Texas Rangers, and it was George who had finally put an end to the career of "Uncle John" Selman while working with Jeff at El Paso. Milton called on Scarborough for help in Arizona while working for Wells Fargo, nominally as an express messenger. While his job primarily called for loading and guarding whatever was shipped, the company knew his reputation and took frequent advantage of his special skills. He was sometimes assigned to go out and find criminals who had stolen from Wells Fargo or, in cases like that of "Bronco Bill" Walters, where the local law enforcement agency asked for help from Milton, they were quick to

J. D. Milton and George Scarborough
(photo by Bushong and Feldmore - El Paso)

grant leave. Since Walters had been a problem for Well Fargo also, they even furnished a railroad car for transporting men and horses quickly in the field.

The hunt for "Bronco Bill" had Jeff and a posse, which included Scarborough, winding through the White Mountains for days. When they finally found the camp that Jeff was sure the outlaws were using as a base, they easily arrested several men, but the main target was not there. They spent the night in the camp, and the next morning while they were seeing to breakfast they heard shots just out of sight. The shooting enabled them to be ready when three riders approached. One was well in the lead of the others and stepped down to talk to one of the first cowboys he saw. These were a couple of the arrested men who were being kept under fairly loose but vigilant scrutiny. One of the men managed to get the message across that they were in trouble, and the newcomer started toward his horse to leave. As he did, Milton called to him, "Hold on there, Cap, I want to talk to you a minute."

The man jumped on his horse and fled, firing back at them. Jeff, who had his rifle ready, shot once hitting the man's extended right arm. The bullet continued through the arm and passed almost completely through his chest, lodging under the man's left arm. He fell from the horse, and Jeff, along with Scarborough, turned to deal with the other two who were still on the other side of a small canyon. Their first shots killed one of the horses, and its rider took to the brush, no longer interested in the fight. The other man dismounted and took cover behind a juniper and opened fire with his rifle. As Jeff told the story, he saw dirt spurt up behind George and asked, "That hit you, George?"

"Never touched me," was the answer just as Scarborough put a bullet into the tree right under the bad man's nose. The impact and flying bark made the man jump back, and as he did he exposed his hips on the other side of the tree and Jeff shot him. The others identified him as one Bill Johnson. The bullet had shattered his hip and deflected upward into his abdomen. He died during the night despite the attentions of the doctor Milton summoned by messenger from Fort Apache. The typically laconic note he sent read, "Send a coffin and a doctor."

The first man shot was "Bronco Bill" himself, and despite the seriousness of his wound he survived to be sentenced to prison, serve his time, and return to work at the same ranch he had left to begin his career as an outlaw. He later died at the hands of that great cowboy killer, the windmill. He fell from the tower of one while greasing the bearings.

Milton later learned that the shots that had allowed the officers to be ready for that fight were caused by Johnson and the other man stopping to shoot a rattlesnake that had startled their horses. After that Jeff refused to kill a snake unless he absolutely had to. That break with Western tradition involved him in a few arguments but, as with any conviction he held, he stuck to it.

Jeff returned to his regular duties as express messenger until he was put out of commission for a long while because of a miscalculation on the part of some bad guys who pretended to be friends. Billy Stiles was sent to tell Jeff that he had a "mining man" who wanted to look at some mineral claims Milton held out in the Quijotoas. Stiles made a definite date so he and his partners would know for sure they could hold up the southbound train for Guaymas, Mexico, without having to worry about dealing with Jeff and his guns. Unfortunately for all involved, except the sick man, Jeff received a telegram advising him that his relief was ill. He would have to skip his customary layover at Nogales and continue on through. He forgot to send word to Stiles about this change of plans.

When the train pulled into Fairbank the five outlaws, led by Burt Alvord, who had once been a deputy sheriff in Cochise County under John Slaughter, were holding some citizens as hostages and cover. They fired into the express car and ordered Jeff and the express agent who was with him to come out. Milton grabbed his sawed-off shotgun but couldn't use it for fear of hitting the hostages, and he had left his Colt on his desk back in the car. Their next volley hit all around him, and several bullets shattered the bone and opened an artery in his left arm. The bandits thought they had him and abandoned their human cover and rushed the train. They were met by a blast from the shotgun that seriously wounded Jack Dunlap and put one buckshot pellet in the hip of Bravo Juan Yoas. Dunlap was down and Yoas fled.

Jeff managed to snag his sleeve and tear it back to the shoulder. He twisted it around his arm in a makeshift tourniquet to stop the spurting. As soon as that was done he passed out on the floor between two trunks. The outlaws continued to fire round after round into the car to be sure he was killed. He had thrown the keys into the pile of packages at the end of the car and now appeared to be dead. They had no way to blow the safe so they left with nothing for their trouble.

After many months of treatment and refusing to have his arm amputated, he finally had some reconstructive surgery that resulted in his left arm being several inches shorter than the right and the fist tightly clenched. The doctor told him that he would never use that hand. Determined to prove them wrong, he "released" himself from the hospital, threw away the brace the doctor had given him, and went about his business. He filled a buckskin bag with shotgun pellets and hung it from his wrist so that it pulled down on his arm and bounced against his fingers as he walked. With each step and bounce he willed his fingers to grasp the bag until he finally recovered full use of the fingers, although the arm was never very strong or very limber due to the loss of bone.

For a time, while he worked on his arm and hand, Jeff spent his time prospecting. He looked for gold, silver, and oil in Arizona and Mexico. He went as far south as the Yucatan and traveled to the tip of Baja California. He never had any real success but always asserted that he had had a lot of fun doing it, so it was all right.

Once during this period he came into Tucson from California and discovered that Burt Alvord, the leader of the gang whose attack on the express car had left his arm crippled, was in town. After capture and indictment and two jail breaks, Tucson was one of the few places Alvord felt fairly safe from the law, and believing that Milton was still on the west coast, he was pretty brave about claiming he was looking for Jeff to kill him. When Jeff heard about this from a gunsmith friend of his, he bought a sawed-off shotgun and went down to the Kelton Hotel to meet some friends for a drink. They sat down to play some cards with Jeff facing the door and the shotgun leaning against the wall close at hand. When Alvord came through the door, Jeff had him covered with the shotgun before he knew what was happening. Milton's friends all joined in a chorus urging him to go ahead and kill the outlaw, almost drowning out Alvord's pleas to be spared. When he didn't appear to be carrying a gun, Jeff grabbed him by the ear and said, "I don't believe I'll shoot him. I'll take him over and let Mr. Buehman shoot him." Then, still holding on to the ear, he marched the protesting man across the street to the photography studio and had his picture made. Then things turned serious, and Jeff told the "bad man" that if he ever saw him again, he would kill him without hesitation.

Milton was later to say, "He had murdered a bunch of men, and I should have killed him. But you just hate to shoot a man when he's hollerin'!"

There is an interesting side note in the fate of William Larkin "Billy" Stiles, the supposed friend who tried to ensure that the gang wouldn't have to deal with Jeff. He was killed in the line of duty in Nevada in 1908, serving as a deputy sheriff under the name William Larkin.

It wasn't until April of 1904 that Jeff Milton settled down to a steady job. At that time in the United States there was no control or limitation on immigration with one notable exception. Immigration of Chinese had been long forbidden by various federal laws from as early as 1868. Jeff was hired by the United States government to be the "Chinese agent" for the Arizona border. The job was evidently designed just for him. There was no one else with the same responsibilities or lack of chain of command. He was sounded out about the job by Sam Webb, the customs agent in charge of the office at Nogales and appointed by President Theodore Roosevelt. He patrolled the border all the way across Arizona to the Gulf of California to stop as much smuggling of illegal Chinese into the United States as he could. He arrested and deported hundreds of illegal aliens every year from then until the job was eliminated in 1932 when he was seventy-one.

At that point, Jeff Milton retired from law enforcement with a small pension and lived out the rest of his life peacefully with his beloved wife Mildred. He had married her when he was fifty-seven years old, and her influence is probably what settled him to one job for those last years. He never moved away from the desert that he loved. He talked freely of the people he had met, the good and the bad. He always avoided questions about the men he had killed or those questions that seemed to him designed to draw him into confirming his courage.

Jeff Milton died on May 7, 1947; he was exactly eighty-five and a half years old. He was a real fighting man, full of honor and integrity. He lived a life of adventure such as few could match or even imagine. J. Evetts Haley, who knew Jeff in his last years and wrote his biography, called him "simply Sir William Wallace on a cow horse."

Jim Roberts

Good Man From a Bad Start

There are conflicts in all periods and areas of history that leave the historian with the problem of trying to determine which side were the "good guys." Sometimes it is not possible to get a consensus. This was never more true than in the case of the "wars" of the Old West. The battles between cattle ranchers and sheepmen and between stockmen and small farmers are the stuff of the western legend. People on both sides thought they were right, and modern apologists defend one side or the other. This was especially true in the case if the Pleasant Valley War in Arizona.

The "war" was in reality a family feud like many others that have occurred in all places and times. The Hatfields and McCoys have become the archetype of such disputes, but there have been many other long and violent disputes such as the Horrell/Higgins and Sutton/Taylor feuds in Texas. They generally share murky or minor origins that often became insignificant or forgotten in the bloody aftermath.

Jim Roberts was caught up in the feud between the Tewsburys and the Grahams in Pleasant Valley, Arizona, in the middle 1880s. He had a small ranch and had been losing cows and believed they were being taken by Graham men. It is possible the Graham faction had already decided that Roberts was siding with their enemies. When his house was burned Jim became actively involved in the dispute.

In August of 1887 Tom Tucker along with seven other Graham riders attacked a cabin on the Tewksbury range and were driven off with three wounded and leaving two dead on the field. Jim Roberts was part of that defense. In a furious gunbattle between groups of shooters it is almost impossible to know who fired any particular shot. It was the same in this shootout except for the case of one John Paine. Paine's horse was killed under him and fell, pining his leg. It was reported that one shot from Robert's rifle took off the Graham rider's ear. When he got free and tried to run, he was killed by Jim Tewksbury.

About three weeks later, while the Tewksburys were camped by an old cabin, Jim Roberts and a group of men held off a raid by Graham men who had ambushed John Tewksbury and Bill Jacobs when they went out early to get the horses. From early morning until dark the firing continued. After nightfall the Tewksbury riders managed to get clear of the cabin and escape in the dark but were forced to leave the bodies of Jacobs and John Tewksbury behind. The attackers let hogs eat the remains.

Two weeks later, Roberts and Jim Tewksbury were attacked in camp just at sunrise. Even though they were still asleep when the shooting started, they were able to open fire from where they lay, killing one attacker and severely wounding another. The remainder of the raiding party gave up. It may be uncertain which side was the "right" side in this conflict; what is not open to question is the effectiveness of Jim Roberts in tough situations.

After the feud finally ended, primarily due to running out of active participants, Roberts was cleared in court of any criminal wrongdoing. His stock was long gone, his house burned down, and he was broke. There was nothing to keep him in Pleasant Valley so he drifted. He eventually found his way to Congress City, Arizona, a copper mining boomtown. His reputation was such that he was approached to serve as deputy sheriff.

When Jim Roberts pinned on that badge he set the course he would follow for the rest of his life. From that day until his death in 1934, he carried a badge of some sort. There are no known stains on that badge or on the reputation of this man who sought out the difficult jobs in law enforcement during his time.

In 1891 he accepted the position of town sheriff, but by that time there was little for him to do. The next year he was offered the post of constable for the entire Jerome mining district. That job seemed to offer more challenge, but he did not count on the problems created by jurisdictional squabbles. It did not take long to discover that, while the need for law enforcement in the area was great, the position he had been given had so little authority that he could have little impact on the problem.

One of the main problems in the area was the town of Jerome. In 1904 the town was still so wild that the town fathers were looking around for an old-style fighting lawman to appoint as city marshal. They wanted a man who could "put a lid" on Jerome. They wanted Jim Roberts. He didn't have to think long about the offer. He was frustrated where he was, and this looked like a chance to clean up one of the last wild towns in the west.

Jim Roberts did clean up Jerome and did a good job of it. When that job was completed to his satisfaction he moved to Clarksdale, Arizona, a "company" town owned by the Val

Verde Copper Company where he served as constable for many years. During that time he also held a special commission from the county as deputy sheriff so that he could operate anywhere in the county.

He was still patrolling Clarksdale the day in 1928 when he saw two men come rushing out of the bank and leap into a car. As they sped away the cry of "the bank's been robbed" was raised. Jim Roberts, as ready for trouble at age sixty-nine as he had been for the past forty years, responded. The bank robbers were driving wildly for the edge of town. They were staying low in the car with the driver's head just up high enough to see where he was going. It was enough.

Roberts pulled the old single action Colt he carried and neatly shot the driver in the head. When the car went off the road and crashed, the other would-be bandit jumped from the vehicle with the stolen money in one hand and his pistol in the other. He started "high-tailing" it for some other place—any other place would do. The constable, for all his years, took out after the outlaw on foot. As the robber ran, he occasionally fired back at his pursuer. He was no danger to anyone trying to shoot on the run like that, and he got no return fire from Jim.

The outlaw's pistol was empty, and it was obvious that the elderly man giving chase was not going to give up. The thief was, perhaps, also thinking of his dead partner and the shot Jim had made through the window of the speeding car and realized that all the old officer had to do was stop and shoot him down.

Whatever went through his mind at the time, the bandit was through. He was out of bullets, out of breath, and out of hope. He stopped and surrendered. Roberts disarmed him and marched him off to jail. Jim Roberts' last real action as a peace officer was over.

Stopping that bank robbery was not the end of his career, however. He continued to patrol the streets of Clarksdale until January 8, 1934. After fifty years as a peace officer he had a heart attack and died. He died in harness, carrying a badge, on duty to the end.

If there were any questions about how he began his life behind a gun, they were surely answered by all those years of dedicated service, skillfully and efficiently delivered. Jim Roberts was, after all, one of the "good guys."

John Slaughter

His Way, the Right Way

He held his horse back a little as the small party of Comanche raiders started after him. He didn't want to discourage the chase. His taller, faster mount opened up the distance between him and his pursuers. When they were spread out like he wanted he pulled the horse into a quick turn and rode back through the startled Indians, firing left and right. It was a game for teenager John Slaughter. As he grew up near Lockhart, Texas, in the 1850s small parties of hostile Comanche made frequent raids on travelers along the nearby San Antonio-Austin road. This gave him many opportunities to draw them into his game. It didn't take long before they recognized John and refused to come out to play.

John Horton Slaughter enjoyed being called "Texas John" in later life in Arizona. He got miffed when acquaintances would bring up the fact that he had been born in Louisiana while his family waited to cross the Sabine River into Texas. His mother, Minerva Mabry Slaughter, was ill from their trip from Mississippi and was several months pregnant. They stopped in Sabine Parish, Louisiana, during the summer of 1841 on the way to land Ben Slaughter, John's father, had taken up along Huston Bayou on an earlier trip. John was born October 2, 1841, and three months later the family finally arrived in Texas.

Ben and his three boys, Billy, Charley, and John, all served frequently as "minute men" in various Texas Ranger units raised for Indian "troubles," and all four served in Texas units of the Army of the Confederacy during the Civil War. During this time John's skill with weapons was honed and his fiery temper showed itself. Perhaps because he was short, a trim five feet and six inches, or because of some inherited trait, he was to become known, not as a man who couldn't control his temper, but as one to leave well alone when he was angry.

After developing a successful ranching operation in Atacosa and Frio Counties in Texas, Slaughter decided to move operations to Arizona and acquired land near Tombstone. His brother Billy was already ranching in Lincoln County, New Mexico, and had become friends with John Chisum and all of that faction who were involved in the Lincoln County War. Although Billy remained rigidly neutral in that conflict, he and consequently, his brother John, became familiar with the principal players. They knew and were visited by Chisum, John Tunstall, Alexander McSween, Billy the Kid, Pat Garrett, and many others.

John Slaughter was still ranching in Texas when, having arranged to run some stock on Chisum land, he met up with Barney Gallagher. There had been trouble between the two before, and Gallagher knew about the gold coins that Slaughter carried in his money belt when he was away from home. John and his crew were moving a herd when Gallagher caught up to them. He told one of the "drag" riders, "You tell that little rat-headed son-of-a-bitch up front I'm here to kill him." The answer was for Gallagher to wait there, and the rider would tell Mr. Slaughter what he had said. Gallagher was so sure of himself that he had his men stand off until he finished with Slaughter.

When the drag rider delivered his message, Slaughter rode toward the rear of the herd at a high lope. As he approached, Gallagher turned his horse to the side so as to have an easy shot with the sawed-off shotgun he had laid across his lap. He sat still, waiting for John to get into range of the shotgun and evidently was reassured by the fact that his opponent's hands were empty and he had not slowed his horse from its lope. He misjudged the little Texan. Just before he came in range of the shotgun, Slaughter drew the six-gun, which he kept in a holster built into the pommel of his saddle and fired once. Stories vary some, the bullet either hit Gallagher in the heart killing him instantly or hit him in the thigh causing bleeding that could not be stopped. Either way, the man who came to kill John Slaughter was dead. It would not be the last time things worked out that way.

Slaughter was a man who inspired loyalty from those who worked for him. He made some enemies, but there were a lot more friends. His treatment of those who worked for him may be inferred from the great respect shown him by the sharecropping families on his San Bernardino Ranch in Arizona. They served the ranch and its owner, their "Don Juan," faithfully. It is, perhaps, best shown by the loyalty of John Swain, who was a slave who had been given to Slaughter before the Civil War and continued to work for him in the Texas and Arizona ranching operations for many years afterwards. Swain learned the ways of the land with ease and became the best tracker and stock handler that Slaughter ever employed.

John Battivia Hinnaut, known to everyone only as "Old Bat," was another ex-slave who worked for John for years. Billy Slaughter in San Antonio had originally hired Hinnaut after the Civil War and, with Billy's permission, helped with John's second drive of cattle to Arizona when he was preparing to move. Also with Billy's permission, "Old Bat" remained in Arizona to work for John. Having learned the skills of a cowboy in New Mexico, he became another of John's most valuable hands. He served as the trail cook, worked stock, stood guard when Slaughter slept on their frequent cattle drives, and generally looked after the health of his employer, who had a poor record when it came to looking after that precious commodity himself.

These two men played important parts in many incidents in Slaughter's life in Arizona. They were with him along with several other cowhands on an expedition deep into Mexico in chase of some stock stolen by bandits and driven south. They found and gathered the cattle and started back north when the bandits appeared, heavily armed and ready to fight. The cowhands with Slaughter found reason to be elsewhere, leaving him with John Swain and Old Bat to stand against the thieves. They headed the stock into a canyon and set themselves to guard its mouth. When the charge of the bandits was met by heavy and effective fire from the shotguns of the three men holding the herd, the bandits took the same way out used by Slaughter's vaqueros.

John Slaughter ranched successfully for a number of years on the 65,000-acre land grant he had purchased in southern Arizona extending down into Mexico, and San Bernardino, his ranch, was well known throughout the area. It did not escape the notice of his neighbors in Cochise County that he quietly but effectively dealt with rustlers and raiders who bothered his people or his livestock. He had a reputation for efficiently taking care of business while strictly minding his own. He was not there very many years before San Bernardino became known as a bad place to steal stock or cause trouble. Consequently, he didn't have as many problems as some of his neighbors.

John Slaughter
(photo courtesy of University of Oklahoma Libraries)

By 1886 the county, especially the towns of Tombstone and Galeyville, was as wild and lawless as ever. The attempts made to clean up the area by vigilante action, United States marshals, the merchants, and the cattlemen had all failed. The very temporary presence of the famous (or infamous) Earps and Wyatt's longtime friend Doc Holliday had done nothing to suppress lawlessness and had certainly sharpened the acrimonious nature of local politics. In that election year the Democratic Party looked for a man to run for sheriff who was both popular enough to defeat the Republican incumbent and who had a chance of making a difference in the atmosphere of the county.

John Slaughter was reluctant to run for office since it meant being away from San Bernardino most of the time. He could not, however, ignore an appeal to duty. The newspaper, the *Tombstone Epitaph*, supported the Republican ticket, printing an editorial shortly before the election which stated, "After the smoke is lifted from the present campaign, the Democratic Party will learn with sorrow that several of their pet candidates are SLAUGHTERED." In the beginning of January 1887, John Horton Slaughter was sworn in as the third sheriff of Cochise County, Arizona. He had done almost no campaigning himself but had won more votes than any other Democrat to that time.

His work had an immediate impact. He had no patience with the local badmen. Since many of them knew him or at least his reputation from Texas and his relentless methods of keeping San Bernardino an unhealthy place for rustlers and outlaws, they simply accepted his invitation to "leave the county" before they got in trouble. Others had to learn the hard way. After dealing with one who didn't leave, John gave this testimony before a coroner's inquest into the death of one Guadalupe Robles, bandit. Slaughter along with Burt Alvord, Tesano Lucerio, and one other man caught up with the outlaw and two confederates. Alvord was a favorite deputy who, unfortunately, later changed sides and was responsible for the attack on a Wells Fargo rail car that resulted in no loot but left John's longtime friend Jeff Milton with little use of his left arm.

> This morning, after daylight, I crawled up to within fifty yards of the men. I asked them to get up. I asked them then if they would surrender. They answered with their guns in their hands. Just at this time, one of the men fired a shot, and knocked the bark off the tree

close to my ear. Just about that time I shot him. About a second afterwards [the deceased] jumped up with a six-shooter in his hand and I said, "Burt, there is another Son-of-a-bitch. Shoot him!" and I shot him. Just after that this man Manuel ran down the Canyon, probably about a hundred yards away, and I said, "Burt there is another Son-of-a-bitch!" and I shot him. As I shot him he fell on his left side. After that I told Burt to follow him down the canyon, and kill him, and I would stay where I was, and watch those two fellows that were there.

They are the hard words of a hard man, a man who was prepared to do what was necessary to accomplish his task. John Slaughter did just that. After his two-year term ended he felt that there was more to do so he ran for a second term, again without much active campaigning. He won that election with a large margin and the very open support of the *Epitaph*. His second term was much like the first, but by its end Tombstone was a much quieter place. He felt he had accomplished what was needed and declined to run again. He went home to San Bernardino and spent the rest of his life minding his own, very extensive business.

Leaving the office of sheriff didn't mean that Slaughter no longer cared about law enforcement in Cochise County. He carried a commission as deputy sheriff from shortly after he left office until his death. For much of that time he was also designated a special deputy United States marshal.

In September of 1898 he saw a rider make a wide swing around his ranch house at San Bernardino. The man stopped one of the ranch hands and talked for a bit so Slaughter went out to see what was going on. Rios, the ranch hand, told John the man wanted to get a horse from him, but he didn't want any "American" to know. He had run down the owner of the ranch thinking to get the sympathy of the worker, but since the people who worked the ranch were almost universally loyal to "Don Juan" he had no luck and went on his way. Rios was on his way to the main house to report when the boss came out to meet him.

Sure now that something was wrong about the man, Slaughter called into town and described the man to someone at the American Customs House and also to someone in the sheriff's office to see if the man was wanted for anything. He received a return call from Judge S. K. Williams ordering him to arrest the man, Arthur (Peg-Leg) Finney. The judge cautioned him that Finney would probably put up a fight and advised Slaughter to kill him if necessary.

Slaughter picked up his rifle, asked Rios and a man named Lloyd Gillman to come with him, and went after Peg-Leg. They found him in a pasture about a mile from the house, apparently asleep in the shade of a tree. He was lying on his right side with his arm and hand partly under him. They came up to him quietly, and Slaughter picked up Finney's Winchester from the ground near him and threw it a few feet away. That done, he told the man he was under arrest. Finney turned only slightly and came up with a cocked six-shooter pointed right at Slaughter's head. John jerked up his .45-.85 Marlin rifle and fired. The bullet hit Peg-Leg's gun hand and went through it into his chest. Almost at the same instant both Rios and Gillman fired. One of their bullets hit him in the head and the other in the hip. John was later to refer to it as the "closest call I ever had."

A corner's jury convened at the ranch and concluded that Arthur Finney had expired from "gunshot wounds inflicted by Deputy U.S. Marshal John H. Slaughter and his assistants,

Lloyd Gillman, and one Rios while in charge of his official duties as such officer." The body was not claimed, and they knew no one to notify so the young Texas outlaw was buried in the little cemetery at San Bernardino. Eventually there would be thirty-three graves, mostly members of the families that worked the land and the livestock on the ranch.

There is, however, another grave there with a story. In December of 1895 a small group of Apaches killed a farmer and his daughter as they hauled a load of grain to town. Then, as spring warmed up, in March of the following year more small raids and killings brought the Army to quiet the problem. Slaughter, by then in his fifties, was still ready to fight. He had scouted for the Army in Indian troubles before, and they knew him and wanted his help. When an expedition was mounted, scouts John Slaughter, Arthur Fisher, and his brother Jess, the foreman at San Bernardino, led it. John also took along a few of the vaqueros who worked for him.

When the Apache camp was found, the attack was made without warning just before dawn. Lt. N. K. Averill with his troops and Jess Fisher fell on the camp from one side just as Slaughter, Arthur Fisher, and the cowboys hit the other. The Indians did not stand and fight but fled into the rocks surrounding the area. As they searched the campsite they found a baby girl, probably less than two years old, and one about five who had been left behind. Slaughter had to hold his gun on one of the party who wanted to kill both of them. The older girl was sent to the San Carlos Reservation where she was adopted and raised. The baby hardly left the crook of Slaughter's arm until he got her home. After some initial hesitation, John's wife, Viola, accepted the baby and Apache May, soon shortened to "Patchy," became a part of the family.

The next few years were happy ones for the Slaughters. Business was going well, Indian and rustler troubles were few, and they delighted in watching "Patchy" grow up. Tragedy changed all that when, in 1900, the little girl was playing near the "scalding pot" in the yard. The pot was used for heating water for washing and for making soap. She got too close and her dress caught fire, and before Jess Fisher could put it out, Patchy was burned too badly to survive. She died as if she knew what was expected from one of her ancestry, saying goodbye to "Don Juan" and Fisher but never crying. It would be many months before the ranch, and especially its owner, would recover. Slaughter spent so much time sitting and staring across the land that Viola began to worry about him. Apache May's was the saddest of the graves in the cemetery at San Bernardino.

John Slaughter finally recovered somewhat from the loss of "Patchy" and continued to run the ranch and his other businesses right up until his death on February 15, 1922, at the age of eighty. He had become increasingly feeble for several years but still was seldom seen without his pistol and, as always, believed he was prepared to meet head-on anything that came to him. He wasn't buried at the ranch near Patchy or even in Tombstone. He had asked Viola to have him buried in the cemetery at Douglas because he was afraid that Tombstone would dry up, and after all his years of handling his affairs alone, he wanted to be buried where there were going to be people around.

The name "Texas John" could not have been given to him simply because he had moved to Arizona from Texas or because he had served for a time in the Texas Rangers. There were far too many former Texans and not a few former Rangers in the vicinity of Tombstone, Cochise County, Arizona Territory, in the late 1800s for that in itself to be notable.

What may explain it was that here was a man who personified the image, even then reaching the proportion of myth, of the rigid, upright Texan who minded his own business and accepted no interference in the way he took care of it.

Sam Sixkiller
Cherokee Lawman

Solomon Copple was likely thinking about the profits he would make when he sold the wagon load of bootleg booze he was hauling from Missouri to the town of Muskogee in the Indian Territory. He had his head down, letting his horses make their way. His shotgun lay on the seat beside him. He could expect to make three or four dollars profit on each gallon he was carrying. He might have been doing the math to calculate his take.

When his horses shied and backed into their traces, Copple looked up to see a short, dark-skinned man standing in the road with an upraised hand. When the bootlegger saw the badge on the man's shirt and his pistol still in his holster, he made a fatal mistake. He reached for his shotgun. The officer's Colt was "out and barking" before the shotgun cleared the wagon seat. Solomon Copple was dead before he hit the wagon tongue. He had the distinction of being the first, although the least famous, of the only two men known to have been killed by Captain Samuel Sixkiller in the performance of his duties.

Sam Sixkiller was a member of the Cherokee Nation, born in the Going Snake District to Redbird and Pamela Whaley Sixkiller. He was schooled at a Baptist mission school. It was good training. His contemporaries remembered him as a well-spoken man whose behavior reflected well on his upbringing.

When the Civil War began Sam was nineteen. The Indian Nations were as much involved and as deeply divided as any part of the country. The many slave owners among the more well-to-do members of the Five Tribes supported the Confederacy while a number of others declared for the Union. Redbird Sixkiller left his son in charge of the family farm and went north to join the Union army. As with many teenagers, peer pressure led Sam into an action he would soon regret. He was caught up in the excitement of his companions and went with them to enlist in the Army of the Confederacy.

Clearer thinking came to him shortly, and he realized that he had made a mistake. He deserted, slipped away, and made his way to Fort Gibson, Indian Territory, which was, by then, in Union hands. At Fort Gibson he found his father, now First Lieutenant Sixkiller, in command of an artillery company. The younger Sixkiller enlisted and served out the war in that unit.

After the war, Sam married and moved to Tahlequah, the capital of the Cherokee Nation. He farmed and worked at various jobs until 1875 when he became high sheriff of the Cherokee Nation. Each district had a sheriff whose duties were similar to a county sheriff in the States. Those sheriffs were responsible to the high sheriff, who was also in charge of the National Penitentiary in Tahlequah. Sam and his growing family settled into life in the capital.

Both Sixkillers, father and son, were well known and respected in the Cherokee Nation: Sam as high sheriff and his father as a justice on the Cherokee Supreme Court. Sam's reputation for efficiency and careful attention to his responsibilities grew. His record, both as administrator for the Nation's law enforcement system and as warden of the prison, was excellent until November of 1878.

It may have been the fall weather or some other stimulant of youthful spirits that started the ruckus. A group of rowdy young Cherokees came riding through town, shooting their pistols and trying to run over anyone unfortunate enough to be caught out in the street. They got all of the attention they could have wanted. The high sheriff mounted up some of his deputies and went after them. When the officer's demands to pull up and surrender yielded only gunfire, Sixkiller gave the order and the posse answered in kind. One young man, Jeter Thompson, was mortally wounded. Before Thompson died, he accused Sam Sixkiller of shooting to kill because of bad blood that had existed between the two for some time.

Sixkiller and the two prison guards and one town police officer that had made up the posse were arrested and charged with the murder of Jeter Thompson. They were tried during the summer of 1879, but the result was a hung jury. In accordance with existing law the charges were then referred to the Council Branch of the National Council of the Cherokee Nation to be investigated and resolved.

In a letter dated November of that year, Ose Hair, the speaker of the National Council, informed D. W. Bushyhead, the principal chief of the Cherokee Nation, of the Council's decision. They found no proof of malpractice in office as charged against the high sheriff. Sam was free to return to work.

Unfortunately, after being without pay for over five months, the Sixkiller family was now in need of money. Sam applied for reimbursement of $355.50 in back pay and $975 in attorney fees. He was turned down. Sixkiller did not give up; he was not the sort to, after all, but that only led to more problems. He was suspended from his position again in June of 1879. This time it was because of his campaign to be repaid.

Sam felt that his reputation and standing in the community had suffered too much for him to continue to live in Tahlequah. He moved his family to Muskogee, in the Creek Nation. Muskogee was a rail and supply center and cattle shipping point for a large area. It was the center for several booming businesses of varying degrees of legality. It was also the headquarters for the Union Agency, the United States government's official representative to the Five Civilized Tribes of Indian Territory.

The Indian agent, a man named Tufts, had recently been authorized to organize a new police force. This group of officers would have authority to investigate crimes and make arrests in all parts of the Territory. In February of 1880 the agent of the Union Agency selected Samuel Sixkiller to be captain of the United States Indian police. There was also funding for the construction of a federal jail in Muskogee. The jail, when complete, became one of Sam's responsibilities. His job was very similar to the one he had held in the Cherokee Nation, but the pay and prestige were much greater. He also held a commission as a deputy United States marshal from Judge Parker's court in Fort Smith and received a salary from the Missouri Pacific Railroad as a special agent. His record and reputation during this tenure were excellent.

He supervised the work of thirty to forty deputies stationed in various locations in the Nations. There was no lack of work for them. As it had been from the earliest days, Indian Territory, with its rugged terrain, fairly low population, and mixed law enforcement jurisdictions, was a magnet for trouble. Livestock thieves, bootleggers, and timber thieves, along with all the problems that followed the railroad towns: the train robbers, gamblers, con men, and ladies of purchasable virtue, kept the Indian police and Sam Sixkiller busy. These problems were aggravated by the difficulties of dealing with whites trying to move onto Indian land in violation of both U.S. federal law and the laws of the Five Civilized Tribes. Sam had plenty to do, and it was not a particularly safe job, either. He and his men had to rely on training, experience, and their weapons. Sam, himself, was involved in a number of shooting scrapes.

Sometimes the dangers were of other sorts and the problems not easily solved by a quick draw and accurate aim. As a railroad center, Muskogee had a large number of ladies whose virtue was malleable for a fee. The establishments where these ladies practiced their ancient profession often became trouble spots where gunplay and crime was rampant. When several new "painted ladies" arrived in town, Agent Tufts gave his captain of police the order to clean up the town and eliminate the problem.

Sam and his men rounded up the "ladies" and established them in new quarters in the jail. By the time they were finished they were convinced that they would prefer a pitched gun battle with the Territory's most dangerous outlaws. After a short stay in the "accommodations" offered by the Union Agency, the prisoners were ready to take the captain's suggestion that other towns might provide a more suitable business climate.

Indian Territory likely never saw a more dangerous outlaw than the Creek freedman Dick Glass. He was bold and deadly in a fight and a careful organizer of crime. He was also a staunch defender of his people.

The freedmen of the time suffered a great deal from the contempt and harassment of those citizens of the Nations who were of part Indian and part European ancestry. These people were known as "mixed bloods" and were frequently among the well-to-do and influential of their tribes. In the early 1880s there was a great deal of conflict along the Creek border with the Cherokee Nation between Cherokee "mixed bloods" and Creek freedmen.

When the Cherokees began raids into Creek lands occupied primarily by freedmen in retaliation for real or imagined offenses committed by the Creeks, Dick Glass took a hand. He had more than one shootout with Cherokees along the border and was seriously wounded at least once. He also commanded a group of Creek freedmen allied with the full blood Creeks against the mixed bloods in what became known as the Green Peach War. It was the largest and most serious of five conflicts between the two groups over the changes that were being brought about in the traditional ways of life.

The other side of Dick Glass appears as the leader of a group of horse thieves and bootleggers who were always ready to use deadly force to protect their enterprises. They made a practice of stealing horses in the Nations and driving them out of the area to sell. With the money from the horses, they bought whiskey, which they brought back and sold in the Territory. After several years of these activities, the rewards for his capture totaled over a thousand dollars. It was enough to attract the attention of a Texas sheriff named Culp and a former constable, Rush Meadows, both from Cooke County, Texas. When they heard that Glass was hiding out in the Arbuckle Mountains not far to their north, they determined to go after him. They did not return to Texas. Even after they had the drop on him, Dick Glass managed to kill them both.

It was not long after this incident that Glass and three other men were seen heading south toward Denison, Texas, in a covered wagon. They were recognized and a message was sent to the headquarters of the federal Indian police at Muskogee. Captain Sixkiller left Muskogee with some of his officers to try to catch them. They didn't arrive in time to stop the men before they crossed the Red River into Texas.

Sam had three police officers and a cattleman from the Cherokee Nation named C. M. McClellan with him. He decided to wait for the bootleggers to return since he was sure they had crossed into Texas for the sole reason of buying whiskey to sell. By this time Glass had become something of a wholesaler who bought and sold by the barrel rather than bothering with gallon jugs. While they waited, Sixkiller hired a local black man to serve as guide and scout. They did not have long to wait.

The scout kept an eye out along the likely trails the group could use with their wagon until he spotted them. He reported to the captain that he had found where they were camping for the night. The officers moved into position along the trail the outlaws would be traveling in the morning and waited. When the wagon appeared it was being driven by one man, Richmond Carolina, while the other three walked along behind. Sixkiller waited until the wagon was close, then stepped out of the brush and called for the men to surrender.

He might as well have told them to run because Glass and the other two behind the wagon, Jim Johnson and Sam Carolina, took off. When Glass tried to shoot back at the officers, Sixkiller fired his shotgun twice. The loads of buckshot slammed into the outlaw. Dick Glass died instantly. While this was happening, Johnson drew and was cut down by the other officers, and Richmond Carolina laid the leather to his team and tried to escape that way. He refused to stop when the other two officers ordered him to, and when they fired he fell into the wagon bed. The range was close and they believed they had killed him.

Sam Carolina had made his escape on foot in the midst of this. He may have been successful because he did not waste any time by trying to fight. He did not get far. The officers caught up with him within about a half mile, and he was forced to surrender. When they returned to the wagon with their captive they got a surprise. Richmond Carolina had not been wounded badly and had made his escape while they were making the other chase. The man had unhitched the team and, without taking the time to get the rigging off, had ridden off with the horses still harnessed together.

Trying to ride this way did not make for fast going, and he was soon caught by one of the members of the posse. The stories vary; it may have been a policeman named LeFlore or the black scout who rode him down and arrested him.

The posse loaded up the two bodies and took them and the prisoners into the town of Colbert. The bodies were formally identified, and both were buried there. The two outlaws still living were taken to jail in Muskogee and then transferred to Fort Smith for trial.

This information comes primarily from an article that appeared in the Muskogee *Indian Journal* of June 11, 1885, under the title:

DICK GLASS GONE

He and a Companion Are
Now Slowly Roasting

The article also reported that there was a $500 reward outstanding for Glass, "dead or alive" and that, "Capt. Sixkiller will apply for it in a few days."

As with every good lawman, not every arrest that Sam Sixkiller made depended on his skill as a gunfighter. The same newspaper carried this story approximately six months after the death of Dick Glass.

A GOOD CAPTURE

Capt. Sixkiller made a slick capture last week at Weber's Falls. He was after Alf. Rushing, alias Ed Brown, wanted for the killing of Jackson Barfield in 1877. Also for the murder of the city marshal of Wortham, Freestone County, Texas. He received information that Brown was working near the Falls and had been for several years. As the Captain and Bill Drew came near the place where Brown was staying, they gathered up a bunch of cattle, and, driving them up, asked for permission to put them in a yard there for the night. The request was granted, and Brown was called from the crib where he was at work to help pen them. While driving them Sam worked around to where Brown was, and throwing down on him, took him completely by surprise, and he could offer no resistance. The cattle were then turned loose. Brown denies he is the man wanted by the officers, but they are certain they have the right party, and he is being held here awaiting the Texas officers.

In September of 1886 the first act of a tragedy played itself out on the streets of Muskogee, Indian Territory. Black Hoyt and Jes Nicholson had been partaking pretty heavily of whatever supply of bootleg alcohol they could find and began to amuse themselves by shooting up the town. The problem became so serious that a concert scheduled for that evening was cancelled because people were afraid to be on the street and attract the notice of the two drunks.

The problem was addressed by the captain of the Indian police, Sam Sixkiller, with the help of a member of his force, Charley LeFlore. They approached the men, and Captain Sixkiller informed them they were under arrest and ordered them to hand over their guns. Nicholson's response was to yell, "Go to hell!" and take a shot at Sixkiller. The bullet only grazed the captain's arm, and the firing became general in the street. When the shooting stopped, Black Hoyt was under arrest and Nicholson had escaped in spite of a badly wounded foot. Sam's injury was only slight. Hoyt was marched off to the jail.

Problems with Hoyt did not end with that arrest. The next day Black's father showed up in a difficult mood and had some harsh things to say to the officers. He concluded by threatening to kill the captain, and into a cell he went as well.

Sixkiller later learned that Nicholson had gone to hide out with a friend of his, a mixed blood Cherokee named Dick Vann. The captain sent one of his officers out to arrest Nicholson and expected the wounded man to be no problem. They had not reckoned with the character of Dick Vann.

When the policeman rode up to the house, Vann came to the door. The officer dismounted and approached him. He said he was there to arrest Jes Nicholson and they would get a doctor to see to his wounded foot as soon as they got to town. As he moved toward the door, Vann drew and cocked his pistol and ordered the policeman to "leave or be killed." After arguing for a minute and pointing out that the law would just be back in force to arrest them both, the officer gave up and rode back to town.

Sam Sixkiller
(photo courtesy of the Oklahoma Historical Society)

When Captain Sixkiller heard the story he reacted with mild disbelief. After all, Vann had been pardoned only months before on a conviction for an assault he had committed on the person of an army captain at Fort Gibson. Sam sent a request to the judge for a warrant for Vann's arrest for hindering a police officer in the performance of his duties.

By the time the officers returned to Vann's place to arrest the men, Jes Nicholson had died from his wound. Vann was taken back and stored in the jail along with Black Hoyt. Black's father, Milo, cooled off after a few days and was released without charges.

Vann's incarceration in the Muskogee jail didn't last much longer. The charge was assault with a deadly weapon on a federal peace officer since both Sixkiller and LeFlore were commissioned as deputy United States marshals. Hoyt's defense, however, was that they were "just shooting at police," apparently an acceptable pastime in the Nation.

A man named Jim Hannon described a later confrontation between Sixkiller and Vann. Hannon told of an incident at a fair when Sam was watching the gate. Vann showed up at the fairgrounds a little worse for having enjoyed deep draws at the whiskey jug. Before Sam let him in, the captain told him he would have to behave. Vann said that's what he intended to do, but Sixkiller continued to caution him and told him that if he acted up the police would throw him in jail. They continued to argue back and forth, getting angrier as they went, until Sam finally did arrest the man and haul him off to jail. It is said that as Sam shoved Vann into the cell, he kicked him. Vann's response was, "Sixkiller, that kick will cost you your life."

On Christmas Eve of 1886, Sam Sixkiller was not feeling well. He wanted to take his family to the Christmas celebration at the Methodist church that evening so he walked over to the drugstore of Dr. M. F. Williams to see if he could get something that would help. Since he was not working, he was not wearing a gun.

The season was being commemorated with a variety of amusements including two days of horse races. Dick Vann and his brother-in-law, Alf Cunningham, were in town for the races and the general celebrating. For them, that also meant some serious work with the whiskey jug. Neither of them had any regard for the law or the men who enforced it.

Cunningham, temporarily on his own, came across Creek freedman and Lighthorseman Tom Kennard standing in front of the Commercial Hotel and drew on him. A bystander grabbed at Cunningham's gun hand and gave the officer a chance to draw his own pistol and "buffalo" him. Kennard took the man's pistol and, instead of throwing him in jail, sent him on his way. It was, perhaps, a generous impulse in keeping with the season, but it was a mistake.

When Cunningham and Vann got back together they started trying to buy a gun. They could not find anyone who would sell one to them so they went into the Mitchell House and relieved Ray Farmer, one of the owners, of his shotgun. Back in the street, they surprised Shelly Keys, the city marshal, covered him with the shotgun, and took his pistol. That confrontation might have led to worse things, but a crowd started to gather and the two went off in search of Tom Kennard to settle their new grudge.

An older grudge intervened. They were looking for the Lighthorseman but, as they reached the Patterson Mercantile Store, they saw Sam Sixkiller coming up the steps onto the platform alongside the building. They rode up to Sixkiller and Vann yelled, "You'll never do that to me again." He cut loose with the shotgun and blasted some holes in Sam's clothes but none in him. Sam fell off the platform and rolled. Cunningham joined in the shooting using the pistol they had taken from the city marshal. Three bullets hit the captain. One shot was directly to the head. He got to his feet and ran around in a little circle and then fell. It was probably reflex, he was likely dead before he dropped to the ground.

The killers left town at the gallop to avoid a pursuit that was not to come. With "Captain Sam" dead there seemed to be no one ready to go up against the two. A reporter wrote that Marshal Keys "changed his coat and hat that he might conceal his identity and looked as though he might like to contract for a cast iron suit of clothes."

Neither Dick Vann nor Alf Cunningham was ever tried for the murder of Sam Sixkiller. The complications of jurisdictions delayed matters just long enough for Vann to get himself killed in a gunfight in Fort Gibson. Alf Cunningham was in jail in Fort Smith on a federal larceny charge, which made things even worse. Now things had to be negotiated between the courts of the Creek and Cherokee Nations and the federal court. When he was finally turned over to the Creek court for trial, he escaped and was recaptured. The capture was, once again, in the Cherokee Nation, and the jurisdictional wrangling began again. He was returned again to the Creek Nation but escaped again and dropped out of sight. That is the last that is known of him.

There were many expressions of sorrow at the loss of a man like Sam Sixkiller. Perhaps the greatest memorial is found in the fact that an estimated two thousand people showed up to pay him tribute on the day of his funeral. Indian Agent Robert L. Owen, who was also a citizen of the Cherokee

Nation, wrote this to the Commissioner of Indian Affairs in Washington:

> Sam Sixkiller died a martyr to the cause of law and order and had the respect and confidence of all the deçent people in the country particularly of Hon. I. C. Parker, U.S. Judge of the District, M. H. Iandels, Pros. Atty., John Carroll, U.S. Marshal. Every newspaper in the territory had the most respectful and complimentary notices of him.

This is taken from a resolution passed by the Muskogee council:

> ...Samuel Sixkiller, captain of the U.S. Indian Police and Deputy U.S. Marshal... [his death] was a willful and cowardly assassination. For seven years he had been captain of the U.S. Indian Police... and as such [was] a vigilant, honest and courageous officer, an acknowledged leader in all perilous enterprises and we regard his unfortunate death as being directly due to his honorable and faithful services against the lawless elements that afflict this country.

Sam Sixkiller's death brought about one good thing. The United States Congress debated, then passed a bill the next year which made it a federal crime to assault or kill an Indian policeman or marshal. That law transferred all authority to try such crimes to the federal district court, eliminating the jurisdictional tangle, at least in these cases.

It was to be just over a year later when the courts and police functions of the tribes were disbanded and federal authority was exerted over all major legal matters, criminal and civil, in the Indian Territory. There were county and municipal officers and courts empowered to investigate and try lesser violations.

Historian Art Burton wrote of this time, "Over the years, many deeds and actions performed by the Indian police and Lighthorse members have been forgotten." It shouldn't be so. The legacy of Sam Sixkiller, and all those who served faithfully in those bodies, deserve to be remembered among the "good guys."

"Bear River" Tom Smith

He Named a Town and Took Its Name

Rage gripped him. The bullets from the guns of the vigilantes ripped through his body, but he wouldn't go down. Charging at the head of an angry mob of railroad workers, he emptied both pistols into the log storehouse. When the fighting was over, fourteen men were dead and many more were wounded. Tom Smith slowly walked to the cabin of a friend before he finally collapsed, near death.

It had started out simply enough: A rail worker, a friend of Tom's, had been enjoying his off work time with a little fun that included a lot of whiskey and some "hoorawing." He did some shooting, but he wasn't hitting anyone. But Bear River, Wyoming, was becoming more of a real town than the usual "end of the track" collection of portable shacks and tents that were taken down and moved every time the rails were extended another fifty miles or so. It was no longer the railroad worker's "hell on wheels." There were some permanent homes and businesses in log structures, and the citizens were beginning to want to put a lid on the more exuberant excesses of the rail hands. They were urged on by editorials in the *Frontier Index*, a newspaper published in a tent that followed the rail camp as it moved. They named themselves a marshal and organized a vigilance committee to deal with the problem.

When the conflict came, the rail workers destroyed the newspaper equipment and emptied the log cabin that was used as a jail. They had just started trying to burn that down when the vigilantes arrived and took cover in a log store building nearby. The townsmen started taking potshots at the railroaders, who had pretty much accomplished what they had started out to do. Everything, that is, except for burning the "jail," which was built of green logs and wouldn't stay lit. That was the way things stood when Smith came on the scene and lost his temper and nearly his life.

Once he had recovered—and it was a slow process because his wounds were many and serious—everyone remembered what happened at Bear River. When the rail camp leaders wanted someone to keep the peace as the "hell on wheels" moved west, they thought of "Bear River" Tom Smith. Even the roughest of the men recalled the blind rage that led that charge, and many of them had seen Tom practice with the pair of pistols he wore. None wanted to challenge him. They may not have realized, and Smith may never have tried to explain, how much he had changed as a result of that experience. The hallmark of the rest of his life was the control of his temper and a quiet determination to avoid having to kill anyone as he enforced the peace.

His reputation spread, and in 1870 he was invited to come to Abilene, Kansas, to apply for the job as town marshal. At that time Abilene was probably the wildest of the open towns of the West. That dubious honor would move as time went on, but for its time there were few contenders for the title with the reputation of Abilene. The young mayor T. C. Henry was being pressured by the permanent and more sedate citizens to do something about the wild behavior of the cowboys "up from Texas" with the herds.

He interviewed Tom Smith, and while he was impressed with his quiet confidence, he was not sure that such a soft-spoken and gentle seeming person could handle the job. That combined with the thought that there was a lot of difference between the man's reputation and his appearance made the decision for him. It would not be a good idea to bring in a man who might turn out to be as wild as the ones who needed to be contained. Besides, it was likely that a man who was known to never back down would just get himself killed right off the bat.

Things got worse. Locals who wanted to try the job were appointed marshal and were not very well treated by the rougher element. The Texas cowboys with the herds were particularly impatient with any attempt to stifle their fun. Lawmen quit one after another, including a couple sent by the St. Louis police chief in response to the mayor's plea for help finding "a couple of good men." That fine pair took the evening train back home the same day they arrived in Abilene.

It must have been something very like desperation that sent the young mayor to the telegraph office to send the wire to Colorado. The response was positive, and late in May 1870 Tom Smith rode into Abilene with the same quiet demeanor and air of determination that had impressed and confused Mayor Henry on the first trip. The mayor, however, still wasn't quite certain. He urged Tom to look the town over before deciding to accept the job. Smith agreed to do that since the mayor wanted it and spent the day looking things over. He returned late that afternoon.

The mayor wanted to know what Smith would do if he gave him the job. The response was frightening both in its simplicity and the seeming impossibility of accomplishment. The problems that couldn't be dealt with by law enforcement stemmed from the fact that a large number of heavily armed men were engaging in serious recreational drinking, and when trouble started, tragedy followed too quickly for anyone to intervene. There was nothing that could be done about the drinking; eliminate that and you eliminated too much of the town's business. That left the guns. The ordinance against carrying them in the city limits was on the books, it just had to be enforced. When asked how he was going to accomplish that when so many others had failed, Tom just repeated that he thought it could be done.

Mayor Henry swallowed his misgivings and administered the oath of office to the quiet man. Smith said he would see about getting some copies of the gun ordinance made and posted the next day, but to start with he wanted to take a look at some of the tough spots. He pinned on his new badge and started for "Texas Town." It 5eems likely that he expected some sort of reception. After all, he had been in town all day, meeting with the mayor and checking things out. It was not the size of town a stranger could be in long without being noticed.

He had not gone far along the main street of the area when he was met by one of the chief tormenters of the earlier law officers, a self-confident and self-proclaimed tough known as Big Hank. Hank had made it his responsibility to see that the streets of Abilene were not burdened by undue law enforcement. In order to maintain that objective, and seeing that a crowd of interested parties was looking on, Hank accosted the new marshal. Just what, he wanted to know, was this new wearer of the city's tin star intending to do about the laws? Tom Smith assured him that he intended to enforce them. What about the gun ordinance? That too, Tom told him. In fact, he might as well start now. He asked Hank for his gun. That did not go over too well, and the bully explained in certain and profane terms that no one was going to take his gun. Tom asked again, still quiet, still calm.

As the second refusal was winding down in a blue streak of four-letter words, Smith stepped in close and brought up one big fist. Hank went down. As Hank recovered his focus, the marshal bent down and yanked the man's pistol from its holster. When the dazed man was able to get back on his feet he looked at the marshal in astonishment, and when he looked into those calm eyes he saw something that did not encourage him to hope for leniency. The order was to get out of town and don't come back. Big Hank suddenly saw the wisdom in that course of action and did what he was told. The crowd scattered and took with it the news that a different sort of lawman had come to town.

The next morning another of those opposed to the idea of putting any kind of lid on a wild town was waiting for Tom Smith. This man, Wyoming Frank, who cowboyed on one of the nearby ranches, had just gotten the news and was determined to take care of the upstart officer. After getting his courage oiled up at one of the many saloons, Frank finally saw Tom coming down the street. He went to meet the marshal and take care of business. He intended to force a gunfight and win it. No marshal, no law, it was simple. Frank stepped out to face Smith, and Tom stepped in close, almost touching the shouting man. Frank backed off a step to get some room to draw, and Tom moved with him. He stepped back again, and again the marshal was right up against him. All the time Smith was asking Frank to hand over his gun, and all the time Frank was trying to get some room to get it into play. They kept moving right through the door of the saloon. Tom asked for the gun twice, as was his custom, and when the cussing and backing continued, the big fist came up again. Two punches and Wyoming Frank was laid out on the saloon floor. The marshal snatched the falling man's gun from the holster and, by the time he hit the ground, was beating him severely across the body with the barrel. When he finally let Frank up, it was with the order to "Git." Frank "got." He didn't even need all of the five minutes he was given to get out of town.

The shocked silence of the men in the saloon was finally broken by the saloonkeeper himself as he offered his own pistol to the new marshal. Then came the inspired move that let the whole issue of the gun ordinance work. "Just check 'em with the bartender, boys, and pick 'em up when you're ready to leave town." No wasted time, no embarrassing trip to the marshal's office, just hand them over at the first place of business you patronize and get them back on the way out of town.

It was not hard to sell the merchants on the idea. They would get a second chance at selling something, whiskey, food, whatever, to each man just before he left. Besides, the peace being created without too much upset on the part of the cowboys was good for business. Even the drovers seemed to accept it pretty well. Perhaps they took some satisfaction from the fact that it took a man of the quality of "Bear River" Tom Smith to hold them down. They began to put some pressure on their friends to conform. No one wanted to be the only one following the rules.

Tom made it easy for them. He was honest, fair, and aboveboard in the way he enforced the law. It took a wheelbarrow to haul off the pocket pistols and derringers that he collected when he visited the "girls" of "Texas Town." No one was exempt from complying with the law. He didn't try to shut down the town. Abilene lived on the cattle trade. The drinking, gambling, and general hell-raising were part of what came with that trade. He just made it safer for the permanent citizens and the cowboys alike to enjoy the proceeds of their hard work.

The town fathers recognized the value of what they had in their law enforcement officer, and when they met in June of 1870 to ratify the mayor's appointment they set the salary at $150 a month plus $2 for each arrest. In August of the same year they decided to raise it to $225 a month. That may have been a record for a western law officer's salary at that time. Some of the townspeople took up a collection to show their gratitude and bought Tom a pair of pearl handled revolvers. This for a man that no one had ever seen fire a shot at anything other than a target. They had, however, seen him target shoot, and it was enough to convince them they didn't want to put the marshal in a position where he had to use those pistols against them.

He spent his time on horseback watching the streets. As the herds came and went for the next few months there were new cowhands to convince that the signs meant what they said. Occasionally, the big fists had to come into play again. From the saddle he was especially effective. The old-timers told stories about some of the ones who resisted, like the one who nearly bit his own tongue off when the blow closed his jaw, and the one who turned a complete back flip when Tom leaned down from the saddle and hit him right in the forehead. Tales like that of bruises and broken ribs drifted down the trail with words of respect for the man who enforced the law. The trail hands were more careful, the hard cases more likely to avoid town, and Abilene grew quieter and more prosperous than before.

Even larger than the truth were the stories of attempts to ambush the marshal and the times he was shot at while making arrests. Some came to believe that he wore a steel plate under his shirt. Others, more superstitious, talked about some magic that protected him from bullets. Through it all, Tom Smith upheld the law and kept the peace, and still the guns came out only for target practice or to lay a barrel across the head of a particularly difficult hard case.

Sometime in the fall of that year Tom Smith resigned as marshal of Abilene. He still lived there but had pinned on the badge of a United States deputy marshal. It was a job with more responsibility and was a tribute to the success he had in bringing order to Abilene. His continuing presence in town must have been a comfort to the citizens.

Out in the country, a dispute over some loose cows and the damage they did to a neighbor's cornfield resulted in a confrontation between John Shea, the owner of the livestock, and farmers Andrew McConnell and Moses Miles. In the process Shea tried to shoot McConnell, but his gun misfired. McConnell had better luck. After Shea's death McConnell turned himself in to authorities and was released after the facts were investigated. It should have ended there.

Friends of Shea's, upset with the result of the investigation, managed to talk a judge into issuing an arrest warrant in hopes of getting McConnell tried for murder. The task of serving the warrant fell on the county sheriff. The sheriff returned from the homestead empty-handed and explained that the accused man was holed up in his dugout cabin. Since the only way in was a narrow trench leading to the door set in the side of the hill, the arrest was going to be difficult. Would Tom Smith please come help him out?

It wasn't the deputy U.S. marshal's job, but Tom wasn't the sort to turn down a request for help from another officer. They rode out to the farm together. When they arrived McConnell and Miles were standing outside the dugout. McConnell moved back into the dark dugout, and Miles waited to meet the lawmen. Leaving the sheriff to handle whatever happened outside, Smith went quickly down the entrance trench to get McConnell. As he disappeared, Miles snatched up an old rifle and pointed it at the sheriff. According to one version of the story, the gun wouldn't fire but the sheriff, evidently not much of a law officer or much of a man, backed away as Miles repeatedly pulled the trigger. There may have been shots exchanged but, in either case, the sheriff left the field.

Two shots, almost together, sounded from the depths of the dugout. The sheriff ran for town, on foot, abandoning his horse and Tom Smith. Another man, no braver than the sheriff, had followed along and hid in some bushes to watch the action. Without him we might not have known exactly how the story played out.

The first shot had been McConnell's as might be expected. He hadn't missed, but this was "Bear River" Tom Smith. A bullet through the body didn't take him down. He fired his only shot at another human being during his time in Abilene, wounding and disarming his attacker. He grabbed the man and started backing out the doorway dragging McConnell with him. As they came into the light Miles clubbed Smith in the head with the butt of his rifle. The two quickly dragged the unconscious marshal out into the open and one of them, it is believed to be Miles, went for the axe.

When Tom Smith's body was found, the head was almost completely severed. One of the best of the "good guys" was gone. Abilene knew it, and the funeral it gave him was a tribute to the man who brought order to a wild cowtown.

His career was short, and there is very little we really know about the man. It is possible that Thomas J. Smith was not even his real name. He was not the man by that name who came from Texas and was involved in the stupid futility of the Johnson County War in Wyoming. It may be true that he was born in New York and served a time as a police officer in New York City, but we are not sure of these things. His recorded career began in extreme and seemingly unjustifiable violence, but surely no man ever so completely redeemed himself by his actions.

Willie Kennard

Tough Enough to Do the Job

"Barney Casewit, you're under arrest." Willie Kennard knew this test would determine whether or not he achieved his dream of becoming a law officer. He was ready for the test.

"I'm just supposed to come with you? Where are we supposed to go?" Casewit and his poker-playing cronies seemed to think this was a joke played for their amusement. After all, he had already killed two town marshals and several other men with no real resistance. He had raped a fifteen-year-old girl and killed her father, a bookkeeper at the bank, when he tried to do something about it. They saw little to fear from the tall slender black man who had just pinned on the city's star for the first time.

Kennard had an answer ready for him. "Your choice, jail or hell."

Like many who thought they were bad men, Barney Casewit wore two guns. When he went for them he learned just what kind of man he was up against. It is difficult for anyone who knows anything about gunfighting to believe what happened.

Bert Corgan, who served as judge because he was the town's only lawyer, described the scene in his autobiography. By Corgan's account Willie Kennard drew and fired twice before Casewit's guns cleared their holsters. The shots hit Casewit's pistols, almost ripping the holsters off the belt. Another account, slightly more believable, says the first shot hit Casewit's right hand and pistol while the gun was still in the holster but he got off one wild shot with his other hand before Kennard's second bullet hit his left arm, taking the fight out of him.

About that time two of the would-be badman's friends decided to take a hand. Kennard dived to one side, rolled and fired, rolled again, and fired once more. Ira Goodrich and Sam Betts were dead. The mayor had made getting the marshal's job conditional on taking Barney Casewit alive. He hadn't said anything about the other two. Besides, there wasn't time not to kill them. The trial was held the next day with Bert Corgan acting as judge. The "bad man" of Yankee Hill was convicted and sentenced. The new marshal was instructed to nail a crossbar on a pine tree behind the blacksmith shop and carry out the will of the court.

The life of a United States Army sergeant was one of responsibility, discipline, and following orders. It was good preparation for a peace officer. Willie Kennard had served in the 7th Illinois Rifles during the Civil War and had been promoted to corporal. During the war his skill with weapons led to his being assigned as an instructor at the Montrose Training Camp. After the war it was hard to find work that suited him so he re-enlisted, this time in the 9th U.S. Cavalry, and served with honor in the Indian campaigns in the West. For seven years he fought against the Kiowa and Comanche in Nebraska, Kansas, and Texas, and stationed at Fort Davis in the Arizona Territory, he saw action against the Mescalero and Warm Springs Apache.

His goal was to make sergeant and he did. When that was accomplished he let his enlistment run out and wandered around for a few months, trying to satisfy his goal of becoming a law officer. He saw an advertisement in a newspaper offering the job of town marshal of Yankee Hill, Colorado Territory, at the dandy salary of one hundred dollars a month. He knew that his army training and experience made him particularly qualified to do that sort of work. All he had to do was to convince the person doing the hiring to consider a black man. In 1874 Yankee Hill was one of the towns the gold rush of 1858 had caused to spring up, and it was a tough one. Getting the job was not made easier by the necessity of convincing the town that a former slave should have such a position, no matter how good he might be at it.

Willie Kennard had successfully carried out his first assignment and earned the respect of most of the townspeople. One version of the story has it that when the mayor told Kennard he could have the job if he brought in Casewit alive, Kennard made a condition of his own. "If I do what I say, you agree to never call me 'boy' again." It seems most of the town found that to be a good bargain.

Unfortunately, it was not enough for some. Reese Durham, manager of the Butterfield Stage station wanted to run the new marshal out of town. In September of 1874, Durham, encouraged by an afternoon of drinking, challenged Kennard. He became a permanent resident of the town's equivalent of Boot Hill.

The following spring a gang of outlaws led by Billy McGeorge began holding up the stages and freight haulers along the trails going through the town. The town council wanted the marshal to go after the hold-up men and put a stop to the robberies. Kennard figured that if he went after them, he would have to chase the outlaws all over the countryside and might never catch up with them. He had wanted posters made up offering a reward of fifty dollars for the capture of Billy McGeorge "dead or alive." McGeorge was furious. In every other jurisdiction where the gang operated the reward was at least three hundred dollars. It was an unbearable insult.

Kennard had arranged for people to watch the roads into town, and when McGeorge and his men rode in to settle with "the law" in Yankee Hill they found him waiting with a double barreled shotgun in his hands. He ordered the outlaws to drop their weapons in the street. Cash Downing decided to try the marshal. The load of buckshot killed him before he could get his gun in action. It also killed the man behind him and blew out a store window. The rest surrendered and were marched off to jail. As they went, McGeorge vowed to have his revenge. Before he got that opportunity, Bert Corgan charged him with the deaths of a family named Stalcup who had been robbed and killed along the trail to the gold mines. He was convicted and kicked out the end of his life on the same pine tree that had claimed Barney Casewit the year before.

Between the efficient work of the marshal and the effects of the gold mining slowing down, Yankee Hill was getting pretty quiet by the next year. Kennard decided it was time for him to move on. He resigned, saying that he wanted to look for a wife back East. Nothing is known of him between 1877 and 1884 when he showed up in Denver working as the bodyguard for Barney Ford, another former slave and by then, a wealthy Denver businessman. After that we know nothing else about Willie Kennard; ex-slave, soldier, and fighting lawman, who left a mark which is almost obscured by history's neglect, but the straight mark of a "good guy" nonetheless.

Bass Reeves
Least Known, Perhaps the Best

Bob Dozier seemed a man destined for success. He had done well as a farmer for several years before he gave that up for a more lucrative career as a criminal in the Indian Territory. His success as an outlaw grew out of his determination to keep his activities well diversified. He robbed stores, banks, cattle buyers, stagecoaches, and even stuck up poker games when he could find one where the money was worth the trouble. He carried out various swindles on land deals and other money exchanges. He headed a ring of thieves who moved about the countryside stealing horses in one area and disposing of them in another. He "fenced" stolen property for other thieves and, in general, got into anything that he could that would make him money without the onus of honest labor. Maybe the reason he was not caught sooner is that the diversity of his victims was such that no single group ever got mad enough to really target him or push the law to get him stopped. The fact that he was known to have killed several men and was known to be the sort who never forgot a kindness or a disservice added to the problems the law had catching him. Anyone who believed Dozier needed to be caught was likely to be too afraid to give information or assistance to the deputy U.S. marshals who were on his trail.

He avoided Judge Parker's men for several years and seemed confident that he could keep ahead of any who came after him. The tall black deputy on the big horse, though, was getting annoying. Every time confederates were able to get word to him, it was the same thing. "Bass Reeves is hunting you." Every time he checked his backtrail the marshal was there, sometimes with a single posseman, sometimes alone. Dozier tried leaving notes along the trail telling his pursuer what would happen to him if he kept chasing him. He left messages with people to warn off the marshal that if he did not let up he would kill him. Bass sent back word that it would suit him if Dozier tried; at least the outlaw would have to stop running to kill him, and he was ready.

Finally, after months of chase and close calls, Reeves had a good, fresh trail and knew he almost had his man. With one posseman to help him, Bass followed Dozier and another outlaw deep into the thickets of the upper Cherokee Nation. Near the end of the day, with success almost in sight, the sky fulfilled the promise it had been lowering over them, and a heavy thunderstorm struck. The tracks were beginning to wash away, and darkness was falling. It looked like Dozier would escape again.

Deputy Marshal Reeves and his man made their way down into the bottom of a wooded ravine, picking their way by the occasional flashes of lightning. They were looking for a place to camp with some protection from the storm. Just as they hit the bottom they were fired on. They both dismounted in a hurry and took cover behind trees. As Bass waited for the next shots to give away the location of their attackers, he saw a shadow slip from the cover of one tree to the next. When the shadow moved again Bass was ready. He fired twice while the man was exposed. The shadow fell and didn't move again. The muzzle flash of his weapon had given away Bass' location, and the other outlaw started firing at him. Bass jerked and fell away from the shelter of the tree, down on his side in the mud.

Only the splatter of the raindrops and the rumble of the thunder broke the silence of the woods. Lightning flashed, illuminating the still body. Finally, the shooter appeared from behind a tree, laughing at his success in eliminating his hunter. He was just a few yards from the body in the mud when that body raised the gun that had remained in one hand and in a booming voice ordered him to drop his pistol. The outlaw froze, then tried to bring up his own gun, but just as it came level Bass Reeves fired. The bullet tore through Dozier's neck and he was dead.

Bass felt that the elimination of Bob Dozier was the high point of his career. If so, it had a lot of competition in thirty-two years of wearing the badge of a deputy United States marshal in the Indian Territory. It was a long career of remarkable exploits performed by a remarkable man. The whole story is made only more amazing when the origins of this great lawman are explored.

There is not much known clearly about the facts of the early life of Bass Reeves. It is probable that he was born in slavery about 1838 on the farm of George R. Reeves near Paris, Texas. George Reeves was not a big plantation owner. He was a successful small farmer who owned of a total of seven slaves. He also served at various times as sheriff and tax collector of Grayson County, Texas. He was a member of the State House of Representatives, a colonel in the Confederate army by virtue of his organizing the 11th Texas Cavalry, and after the war, again served in the House and eventually became Speaker.

When and how Bass Reeves left his owner's service is not certainly known. In an interview and in talking to one of his coworkers, Bass said that he served as body servant to Colonel George Reeves during the war and was at the battles of Chickamauga, Missionary Ridge, and Pea Ridge. His own family's stories as handed down, however, say there was a falling out between master and slave, which led Bass to give George a thrashing; he "laid him out cold with his fist and then made a run for the Indian Territory across Red River."

The stories do not tell when this might have happened, and the version given by Bass may have been designed to keep tensions down between himself and the many Southerners with whom he served in the marshal's service. It is possible that some combination of the two descriptions might be right.

No matter what was true of his earlier days, in 1875, when Bass was recruited to work under the court of Judge Isaac Parker of the Western District of Arkansas to serve papers and make arrests in Indian Territory, he was a man who knew the Territory. He was fluent in the Creek language and could make himself understood in the languages of several of the other tribes. He was good with firearms and was a physically strong, imposing, hardworking family man known for his integrity. Descriptions of him by his contemporaries always mention his booming voice, wide grin, and easy laugh. He was the kind of man who had confidence in himself and lived accordingly. In the early days a deputy was paid only on a system of fees for bringing in prisoners named in the warrants the officer was issued. It is not likely a man like Bass Reeves would have doubted his ability to earn a good living under an arrangement like that.

During most of this time a deputy marshal went out with a pocket full of arrest warrants, one or two helpers to serve as

Bass Reeves
(photo courtesy of the University of Oklahoma Libraries)

guard and cook, and a wagon that served to haul supplies and sometimes the prisoners. Some folks called it the tumbleweed wagon, as it rolled from one place to another, stopping briefly here and there to pick up another unwilling passenger. If the men arrested were unwounded and otherwise sound, the marshal might very well march them alongside the wagon to save the strain on the team.

Depending on the warrants they had to serve, the deputies usually had thirty days to make the trip, out and back, from Fort Smith. Sometimes they would go as far as Fort Sill, almost four hundred miles. They were paid a two-dollar arrest fee plus seventy-five cents a day and ten cents a mile for each prisoner they hauled and out of that had to keep them fed. In the rare case of there being a reward offered, they got that as well. In fact, unless there was a "wanted, dead or alive" reward out for an outlaw, the deputy got nothing at all for bringing in a dead body. This meant shooting to kill only paid off when it was necessary to save a deputy's skin.

This was the kind of life Bass Reeves took on when he accepted the badge and became one of "the men who rode for Parker." The next thirty-two years are full of the stories that might have made another man a legend; stories that deserve to be told; stories that make Bass Reeves one of the real "good guys."

Take this example from the summer of 1884. Jim Webb was foreman of a big ranch in the southern part of the Chickasaw Nation that belonged to Billy Washington and Dick McLish, a prominent member of the Chickasaws. Webb ran the place and the forty-five or so cowboys who worked it with an iron will and an even harder hand. Anyone who opposed him found him just as willing to use his gun as his fist.

One of the Washington-McLish spread's neighbors was Reverend William Steward, a black circuit-riding minister who operated his small place as he had time for it along with his preaching. One day Reverend Steward had the misfortune to let a fire get away from him when he was doing some burning, and the resulting grass fire burned over on range that was Jim Webb's responsibility. Webb went to the minister to complain and in the argument that followed, killed him.

Webb was charged with murder, and the warrant fell to Bass Reeves to serve. He took a white man, Floyd Wilson, as posse and headed into the Chickasaw Nation. In order to get close enough to make the arrest without a fight, Bass had both of them dress as working cowboys and simply ride up to the ranch. They got there about 8 o'clock in the morning, and like any drifters looking for work would, they asked if they could have some breakfast.

There were only three men at the ranch house: the cook, a man whose name they later learned was Frank Smith, and one other that Bass was sure was Webb based on the descriptions he had been given. Smith and Webb told them to "come on in" with apparent unconcern, but both men kept their pistols in their hands, giving the vivid message that they were suspicious and ready for trouble.

Reeves had about decided the two men had accepted their story when the cook called them to the table and he and Wilson weren't followed. Then, through the doorway, he saw Webb whispering to Smith and waving his hand in the marshals' direction. Bass took advantage of the moment to tell Wilson that he thought the men intended to kill them and that Wilson should take Smith while Bass took care of Webb.

When they were through eating they joined the other two on the porch and took seats on a bench as indicated by Webb.

With Webb and Smith standing over them, pistols still in their hands, Reeves began talking about anything and everything, keeping his attention focused directly on Webb's face so that the outlaw had no chance to give his partner a signal to start the action. As Bass talked and hoped for a break, he got the kind that could only be expected in stories. Webb's attention wandered for just a second, but it was enough for Reeves to grab Webb's throat with his huge left hand and poke his revolver in the man's face. Webb was busy trying to force words of surrender past the fingers gripping his windpipe, but Smith was drawing his gun. Reeves' move had been so sudden that Wilson froze. Smith got off two wild shots before Bass could turn and shoot him in the stomach.

The marshals hitched up a wagon and started for Fort Smith. By the time they reached Tishomingo, the Chickasaw capital, Frank Smith was dead so they buried him there and hauled Jim Webb off to appear before Judge Parker. That case was apparently settled. But, as is so often true, things did not turn out that way. Bass Reeves was not through with Jim Webb yet.

After about a year in jail in Fort Smith while his friends and lawyers managed to hold off his trial date, two of those friends, Chris Smith and Jim Bywaters, managed to come up with the $17,000 necessary to get Webb released on bail. Of course, when the trial came, Jim Webb was nowhere to be found. It may be supposed that his friends were confident of his ability to repay their assistance.

When Bass Reeves tracked him down on the fugitive warrant, the trail led back to the Chickasaw Nation to where the present town of Woodford, Oklahoma, is; it was then known as Bywater's Store. It belonged to that same Jim Bywaters who had lost the bond money when Webb failed to appear.

This time there was no chance of not being recognized so Reeves sent his posseman, John Cantrell, ahead to see if Webb was at the store. When Cantrell saw Webb sitting by an open window he signaled to Reeves to come on. As he rode in, Webb saw him and jumped though the window with his rifle in his hand and headed for his horse. The deputy had the angle on him, and Webb saw that he could not get mounted before he was caught. He turned and headed for the cover of some brush. He had no intention of letting himself be returned to jail and the not-so-tender mercies of the man in Fort Smith known as the "hangin' judge."

When Webb realized he couldn't make it to cover either, he stopped and opened up with his rifle, determined to kill the man chasing him. He fired as fast as he could jack shells into the Winchester and was making a pretty good show of it. Bass was involved in some fancy riding at the time since his horse had been startled by the first shots, got his head down, the bit in his teeth, and was crow-hopping in mighty bounds directly toward the outlaw. One bullet cut a button off of Bass' coat and another cut his reins. When that happened there was no hope of getting the animal under control so Bass jumped off the best way he could and hit the dirt rolling.

As Reeves remembered it, Webb shot four times, each time running a little closer. The last shot went through his hat brim as he came out of the roll. Bass came up with his rifle in his hands and, as he did, got off two quick shots. Webb dropped. As Reeves approached him so did both Cantrell and Bywaters. Webb was lying with his pistol now in his hand, and Bass called for him to throw it away. After a brief hesitation the outlaw weakly tossed the gun away from him. The three men approached in time to hear Webb's last words. This is what he said as recorded later by Jim Bywaters.

"Give me your hand, Bass. You are a brave, brave man. I want you to accept my revolver and scabbard as a present, and you must accept them. Take it, for with it I have killed eleven men, four of them in the Indian Territory, and I expected to make you the twelfth."

Bass said later that when he got to Webb's side he saw that his two shots had struck in the middle of the man's chest about half an inch apart. He estimated the distance at about 500 feet.

They buried Webb there near Bywater's Store and took his boots as well as the gun and holster with them to show that they had carried out their commission. Bass Reeves evidently kept the pistol as requested. Reeves and Cantrell then met Deputy J. H. Mershon, who was also in the area, and headed back to Fort Smith with a load of prisoners. The following is taken from a newspaper article in the *Fort Smith Elevator* of July 11, 1884:

A Trip Not Entirely Devoid of Interest

We mentioned last week the arrival of Deputy U.S. Marshals J. H. Mershon and Bass Reeves with a load of prisoners from the Choctaw and Chickasaw Nations. We find them registered at Jailer Burns' office as follows: Cash Benton (white), Robert Colbert (Indian), Eli Riddle (negro), assault with intent to kill; Sterling Williams, A. P. McKinney (negroes), Joquis Thawes, Ike Ross, George Seeley (Indians), Ed McCurry (white), larceny; Thomas Logan, Wash Taylor (negroes), Colbert Moore (Indian), J. D. Williams (white) introducing and selling whiskey in the nation. Colbert Moore immediately gave bond. Ed McCurry is badly wounded in the groin, having made such a vigorous resistance when arrested that the officers were compelled to shoot him. The Indian police made his arrest. In the fight, Ed's partner was killed and one of the policemen was wounded in the knee. He is charged with peddling whiskey in the Territory and also with larceny. He was brought all the way from near Tishmingo lying on a mattress, in the bottom of a wagon bed, and stood the trip remarkably well considering the severity of his wound. On the trip the Marshals killed a man named Webb who was charged with murder and would not submit to having the writ served on him. Near Fishertown, Mershon attempted to arrest one Hamilton, a full-blood Creek Indian, on a charge of murder, when he resisted by firing on the officer and his posse and running. In the melee Mershon's horse fell with him, and the posse coming up at full speed behind, ran over the prostrate man and horse, bruising them both up considerably, while Hamilton escaped to the woods, where the officers learned he soon afterwards died.

Being a U.S. Marshal may appear to some a regular picnic, but we don't want any of it in ours.

Time after time articles like that can be found in the territorial papers, those of Fort Smith, Arkansas, and Paris, Texas, where Bass was stationed for a while. They often just list in laconic detail from a half a dozen to a score of malefactors brought in to face judgement.

It was while working out of Paris that Reeves was given a warrant for the arrest of one Tom Story, horse thief extraordinary. Story had led a gang for several years that made a business out of stealing horses in the Indian Territory and driving them across the Red River to sell them in Texas. In 1890 they tried something different and went down into

Texas and stole a herd of horses and mules from a rancher named Tom Delaney.

Delaney had learned who had his stock, sworn out the warrant, and was evidently eager to recover his animals. He was eager enough to sign on with Bass as his posse. The marshal's plan was to catch Story as he returned to Texas. They would wait along the trail where the horse thief had crossed into the Chickasaw Nation at Delaware Bend Crossing near where Interstate 35 crosses the river today.

They camped back in the trees and underbrush a short distance away from the trail but near the river. They fished, hunted, and took it easy for four days until word came to Bass from an informant that Story was on his way. He was coming back to Texas with a couple of Delaney's mules that had not sold, and he obviously didn't expect a welcome back party. When the deputy marshal stepped out of the brush and announced he had a warrant for Story's arrest the man reacted.

Whether he knew who he was facing or what the odds were is not known because when he saw Bass's pistol still in the holster and went for his own the party was over. Tom Story didn't even get his six-gun into action before Bass's bullet ripped through his body; he wasn't alive when he hit the ground.

They buried Story there. Delaney took his mules home, and Bass reported back to the marshal's office at Paris. The Story gang was finished without its leader and was no longer a problem in Texas or the Territories.

It was not much later when Bass, then working again out of Fort Smith, had dealings with one of the worst badmen of the time. The newspaper *Vinita Chieftain* carried an article on November 27, 1890, giving some details of an attack made by a posse led by Bass Reeves on the home of Ned Christie. This started a double crosscurrent of rumor and misinformation. First the posse believed, and reported, that Christie had died in the fire. This not only proved to be wrong but old Ned was promising to get even with every man in the party that attacked him. Shortly after that, reports started circulating that Christie had killed "the well known Deputy U.S. Marshal Bass Reeves." These rumors bounced around for nearly a year.

After reports of his death appeared in a number of different papers, this clipping, probably from Eufaula, where Bass was very well known, hands out some first-hand information.

It is reported in the Republic from Tahlequah and in the Dallas News from Muscogee that Bass Reeves was killed Saturday near Tahlequah, while attempting to make an arrest. It is thought here that it is a mistake, as Bass was in Eufaula last week and with two wagons and supplies for several days and went west.

Not long after that the Eufaula paper printed this:

Deputy Marshal Bass Reeves lacks lots of being dead, as was reported. . . He turned up Saturday from the west with two wagonloads of prisoners going to Ft. Smith.

While there are many stories from the records of life in old Indian Territory about Bass and his abilities in a gunfight, there are also stories about his skill as a detective. He was quoted as saying he was proudest of the cases he solved by going "undercover." He was known for the disguises he used to trip up criminals. He might appear as a drifting cowboy, another outlaw, a farmhand, or a tramp on the move. It often worked for him but seldom as well as the time he went after two brothers who were wanted badly enough to make them worth $5,000 to the man who brought them in.

The deputy took a small posse with him to the southern part of the Territory, near the Red River, where he suspected the men were being hidden on a farm belonging to their mother. In order to check things out and get his plans together, they set up camp about twenty-eight miles from the farm where he expected to find the men.

He decided to pretend to be a tramp and see what he could learn. He dressed in ragged clothes, knocked the heels off of a pair of old shoes, and shot three holes in the brim of a disreputable-looking hat. He hid away his gun, badge, and two pairs of handcuffs and walked the twenty-eight miles to the farm.

When he got there, he must have really looked the part of the story he told the woman who met him. He "let" her find out from him that he was running from a posse who had put the holes in his hat and asked her if she would give him something to eat. She took him in and fed him, and when he asked to stay and rest a little longer, she suggested that he join forces with her two sons, who were also wanted by the law.

After sundown, a whistle came from the dark, and the woman went out on the porch to answer. Within a few minutes two men rode up to the house to talk to her. Finally, she brought them in and introduced them to Bass as her sons. She explained her idea that the three should work together for mutual protection and profit. They all agreed and decided it was time to get some rest. When they offered the marshal a room of his own to sleep in he offered the suggestion that they stay together in case something happened so they could watch out for each other. This seemed like a good idea so the boys made pallets on the floor while Bass, politely, was given the only bed.

Bass watched the two until he was sure they had fallen asleep, then he slipped out of his bed and very carefully got the handcuffs on them. When morning came, Bass rousted his roommates from their sleep and announced that it was time to get going. It was obvious now that he was not the man he had seemed the night before. Reeves marched them the entire twenty-eight miles back to his camp, the first three miles in the company of their mother, who followed that far, cursing the deputy for all she was worth.

Another time he was on the trail of four outlaws who had held up the Wewoka Trading Post, owned then by Governor John F. Brown Jr., the chief of the Seminole Nation. He trailed the men to Keokuk Falls, one of the towns on the Seminole Nation's border with Oklahoma Territory. It was one of several towns that existed primarily as a center for saloons to cater to residents of the dry, by federal law, Indian Territory. They were wild and nearly lawless places that even the deputy U.S. marshals avoided.

Reeves asked around town in the saloons and learned that his quarry had been there the night before and it was thought they were heading eastward into the Creek Nation. Bass was soon on their trail again. As he followed he came upon an old log cabin that had obviously been abandoned for some time. In spite of the deserted look of the place there was smoke coming out of the chimney. Bass withdrew and the next morning disguised himself as a sharecropper, renting a pair of ancient oxen and a worn-out old wagon. When he was right by the cabin he managed to get the wagon "high-centered" on a stump.

When it seemed obvious to the outlaws that he was unable to get the wagon free, they began to worry that he would bring other help and, perhaps, draw attention to their hiding

place. They feigned helpfulness but acted out of self-preserva-
tion when they came out and began to lift the wagon off of the
stump. Reeves let them. Just as they set the old wagon down,
Reeves stepped back and reached into the pockets of the ragged overalls he wore. When the big hands reappeared they
each held a Colt six-shooter whose muzzle did not waver, and
they realized that this man was not the sort they had thought.
When Bass had them disarmed, cuffed, and chained to the
wagon he loaded up the stolen goods and money from the
cabin. Then they started back to civilization. Bass rode in the
wagon with the four owlhoots trudging ahead of him all the
way to the county seat, about thirty miles. They were eventually transferred to the federal lockup at Guthrie and
convicted.

There is no action taken by Bass Reeves that so illuminates
his personal integrity and commitment to the law as this incident from late in his career. He was living in Muskogee and his
son, Benny, was married and living there, also. Benny's work
kept him away from home a great deal, and this seemed to
have put pressure on his marriage. The situation came to a
head the day Benny came home and found his wife with
another man.

Feeling responsible because of being gone so much, he for-
gave his wife. They worked on restoring their marriage, and
to create a better home life, Benny took a different job which
would allow him to be home more. Things improved and the
couple seemed, once again, to be happy.

During this time, Bass and Benny were having a drink
together and Benny told his father about what happened and
asked what he would have done. The answer came quickly,
"I'd have shot the hell out of the man and whipped the living
God out of her."

It was not long after that conversation that Benny once again caught his wife in compromising circumstances and this time lost control completely. The man got away without damage beyond some scrapes and bruises, but when the rage subsided, Benny's wife was dead. When he realized what he had done, he followed the example of so many others and fled to the hills to escape the consequences of his actions.

When the warrant was issued there were no volunteers; the deputies had too much respect for Bass to want to be the one to go after his son. Marshal Bennett couldn't decide what to do; the warrant had to be carried out, but he was anxious that it be done carefully so that young Reeves would be brought in alive. The deputies felt that even though the behavior could not be excused, it was, at least, understandable.

Bass solved the problem himself. He reported to the marshal's office and insisted on being given the warrant. Perhaps feeling that his reaction had contributed to what happened, he told Marshal Bennett that it was his responsibility to bring in his son.

It took almost two weeks, but when Bass returned to Muskogee it was with Benny in tow. The young man admitted his guilt and maintained his dignity throughout the trial and was tried, convicted, and sent to the federal penitentiary at Leavenworth, Kansas.

Bass stood by his son through the entire time. When the circumstances surrounding the murder became more widely known in Muskogee, petitions were started seeking a pardon. This effort along with Benny's own behavior in prison resulted in a full pardon. He came back to Muskogee and was well known as a barber.

Bass Reeves continued his service as deputy U.S. marshal up until November 16, 1907, the day the Oklahoma and Indian Territories became the State of Oklahoma. He was sixty-nine years old, and thirty-two years of life on the trail of owlhoots had left him with some health problems. He was apparently not ready to stop working, he just wanted to stay closer to home. He took a job as a foot patrolman with the Muskogee Police Department. This report of his hiring comes from the newspaper the *Western Age* from Langston, Oklahoma:

Negro Deputy U.S. Marshal: A Policeman

Muskogee, Okla., Jan. 2 – Former Deputy United States Marshal Bass Reeves a giant Negro, who was in many battles with outlaws in the wild days of Indian Territory and during Judge Parker's reign at Fort Smith, is on the Muskogee police force. . . He is now over 70 years old and walks with a cane. . . He is as quick of trigger, however, as in the days when gunmen were in demand.

The stories from that time indicate Reeves was no less cautious on the street than he had been on the trail. It is said that he was constantly on his guard, wore his six-gun on his hip and another pistol in a shoulder holster, and even that he had a man who went along with him carrying a satchel full of pistols just in case they were needed. After a couple of years of this, his health had deteriorated to the point that he had to give it up. He was very proud, however, of the fact that, according to him, no crime of any sort had been committed on his beat while he was a city policeman.

This article appeared in the *Muskogee Times-Democrat* on November 19, 1909:

Bass Reeves, a deputy United States marshal in old Indian Territory for over thirty years, is very ill at his home in the Fourth ward and is not expected to live. Reeves was a deputy under Leo Bennett in the last years of the federal regime in Oklahoma, and also served in the old days of Judge Parker at Fort Smith. In the early days when the Indian country was over-rid[d]en with outlaws, Reeves was sent to go through the Indian country and gather up criminals who were tried at Fort Smith. Their trips lasted sometimes for months and Reeves would herd into Fort Smith, often single handed, bands of men charged with crimes from bootlegging to murder. He was paid fees in those days that sometimes amounted to thousands of dollars for a single trip.

The veteran [N]egro deputy never quailed in facing any man. Chief Ledbetter says of the old man that he is one of the bravest men this country has ever known.

He was honest and fearless, and a terror to the bootleggers. He was as polite as an old-time slave to the white people and most loyal to his superiors.

His son shot and killed his own wife and Reeves, enforcing the law, arrested his own son. The young [N]egro was sent to the penitentiary.

While the old man is slowly sinking, Bud Ledbetter, who for years was in the government service with Reeves, is caring for the old man the best he can and is a daily visitor at the Reeves home. Police Judge Walrond, who was United States district attorney while Reeves was an officer, also calls on the old [N]egro.

"While Reeves could neither read or write," said Judge Walrond today, "he had a faculty of telling what warrants to serve any one and never made a mistake.

Reeves carried a batch of warrants in his pocket and when his superior officer asked him to produce it the old man would run through them and never fail to pick out the one desired. . . "

Two months later, January 12, 1910, the great lawman was dead. His obituary appeared in the *Muskogee Phoenix* the next day. It is impressive to think that, given the tenor of those times, a former slave could have received this level of attention from the press.

BASS REEVES DEAD;
UNIQUE CHARACTER

Man of the "Old Days" Gone
Deputy Marshal Thirty-Two Years.

Bass Reeves is dead. He passed away yesterday afternoon about three o'clock and in a short time the news of his death had reached the federal court house where the announcement was received in the various offices with comments of regret and where it recalled to the officers and clerks many incidents in the early days of the United States court here in which the old [N]egro deputy figured heroically.

Bass Reeves had completed thirty-five years service as deputy marshal when, with the coming of statehood at the age of sixty-nine he gave up his position. For about two years then he served on the Muskogee police force, which position he gave up about a year ago on account of sickness, from which he never fully recovered. Bright's disease and a complication of ailments together with old age, were the causes of his death.

The deceased is survived by his wife and several children, only one of whom, a daughter, Mrs. Alice Spahn, lives in Muskogee. His mother, who is eighty-seven years old, lives at Van Buren, Arkansas, where a sister of his also is living.

The funeral will be held at noon Friday from the Reeves home at 816 North Howard Street. Arrangements for the funeral had not been completed last night.

BASS REEVES' CAREER

In the history of the early days of Eastern Oklahoma the name of Bass Reeves has a place in the front rank among those who cleansed out the old Indian Territory of outlaws and desperadoes. No story of the conflict of government's officers with those outlaws which ended only a few years ago with the rapid filling up of the territory with people, can be complete without mention of the [N]egro who died yesterday.

For thirty-two years, beginning way back in the seventies and ending in 1907, Bass Reeves was a deputy United States marshal. During that time, he was sent to arrest some of the most desperate characters that ever infested Indian Territory and endangered life and peace in its borders. And he got his man as often as any of the deputies. At times he was unable to get them alive and so in the course of his long service he killed fourteen men. But Bass Reeves always said that he never shot a man when it was not necessary for him to do so in the discharge of his duty and was forced to do it.

Reeves was an Arkansan and in his early days was a slave. He entered the federal service as a deputy marshal long before a court was established in Indian Territory and served under the marshal at Fort Smith. Then when people started to come into Indian Territory and a marshal was appointed with headquarters in Muskogee, he was sent over here.

Reeves served under seven United States marshals and all of them were more than satisfied with his services. Everybody who came in contact with the [N]egro deputy in an official capacity had a great deal of respect for him, and at the court house in Muskogee one can hear stories of his devotion to duty, his unflinching courage and his many thrilling experiences, and although he could not write or read he always took receipts and had his accounts in good shape.

Undoubtedly the act that best typifies the man and which at least shows his devotion to duty, was the arrest of his own son. A warrant for the arrest of the younger Reeves, who was charged with the murder of his wife, had been issued. Marshal Bennett said that perhaps another deputy had better be sent to arrest him. The old [N]egro was in the room at the time, and with a devotion of duty equaling that of the old Roman, Brutus, whose greatest claim on fame has been that the love for his son could not sway him from justice, he said, "Give me the writ." and went out and arrested his son, brought him into court and upon trial and conviction he was sentenced to imprisonment and is still serving the sentence.

Reeves had many narrow escapes. At different times his belt was shot in two, a button shot off his coat, his hatbrim shot off and the bridle reins which he held in his hand cut by a bullet. However, in spite of all these narrow escapes and the many conflicts in which he was engaged, Reeves was never wounded, and this notwithstanding the fact that he said he never fired a shot until the desperado he was trying to arrest had started the shooting.

Hundreds of people, black, white, and Indian, attended the funeral to pay tribute. Unfortunately, history has not been that generous. One of the only references from the early days aside from official records and newspaper articles was found in a history of the Indian Territory, which was written by D. C. Gideon and published in 1901. Gideon wrote:

> Among the numerous deputy marshals that have ridden for the Paris, Fort Smith and Indian Territory courts none have met with more hair-breath escapes or have more hazardous arrests than Bass Reeves, of Muskogee. Bass is a stalwart [N]egro, fifty years of age, weighs one hundred and eighty pounds, stands six feet and two inches in his stockings, and fears nothing that moves and breathes. His long muscular arms have attached to them a pair of hands that would do credit to a giant and they handle a revolver with ease and grace acquired only after years of practice. Several "bad" men have gone to their long home for refusing to halt when commanded to by Bass.

There can be little doubt that more would have been written about him during later times if he had not been black. His time and place of service, while it was difficult for an ex-slave to make his way in a world dominated by whites, was perhaps the only area and period in which he could have made such a career. The people of the Indian Nations were more accepting of blacks than were the many Oklahoma Territory settlers from the East. Those who had emigrated from the South were the least tolerant of all and fueled the push to put laws on the books for the new state that would make the separation of the races a matter of statute. Jim Crow soon ruled Oklahoma, and the contributions of men like Bass Reeves were forgotten. It is time to remember.

The story of Bass Reeves has been obscure and scattered references until more recent times. He deserves better. Art Burton, the man most responsible for bringing together the information revealing the career of Bass Reeves, makes a convincing case, in his book *Black, Red, and Deadly*, for crowning Reeves the greatest of the western gunfighting lawmen. His record of arrests, his skill with weapons, his abilities as an investigator, and his reputation for tenacity and personal integrity combine to make him a striking candidate for that honor. These are all the more impressive when viewed from the standpoint of the disadvantages suffered by a freed slave during the last quarter of the nineteenth century and the first decade of the twentieth.

Over the years there can be found article upon article in the newspapers of the Territory, Fort Smith, Arkansas, and Paris, Texas, announcing that Bass Reeves, sometimes alone, sometimes with other deputies, had arrived with a load of prisoners arrested on his rounds and brought in for justice. These articles usually listed the names, ethnic origins, and crimes of the men brought in. Based on these, and knowing that all of them have not been found, it is not hard to believe the assertion of Bass Reeves that he had arrested over three thousand people. He would add, if pressed, that there were fourteen that he had to kill because they just would not be arrested. He claimed, and the investigations that were conducted bear out, that he never killed unless it was absolutely necessary. In fact, he always said that he never started the shooting. Of course, he did have to finish it sometimes. Bass Reeves was perhaps, the greatest "good guy" of them all.

Bill Tilghman

One More "Good Guy"

To those who know the history of law enforcement on the frontier, it may seem strange that the name of William Matthew Tilghman Jr. has not made a bigger splash than it has so far in this chronicle. There is a reason for that. It has nothing to do with his qualifications as a member of this group. It is just that his story is a little better known than these others are.

After all, he was at one time part of that famous group that enforced the law in Dodge City. He was one of the embarrassed recipients of the specially made and mostly useless Buntline Special Colts. He was certainly the best known of The Three Guardsmen after he became deputy United States marshal for Indian Territory and then Oklahoma Territory. He cannot be left out, but a brief reminder of his legacy should suffice to mark his place in this listing.

He was raised on a farm but looked west to adventure. He was only sixteen when he and some cousins headed west from Atchison, Kansas, to become famous buffalo hunters. The cousins did not stay on the frontier but Bill did. When the buffalo became too scarce to make meat contracts for the railroads profitable, he rounded up open range cattle at five dollars a head. He hunted the almost wild cattle across southwestern Kansas and the Cherokee Outlet and drove them to the railhead at Dodge City.

When he started hunting buffalo, he made a number of influential friends among leaders of several of the plains tribes. When the buffalo were about gone and the tribes realized the animals were being hunted to extinction by the white hunters, that friendship ended, as did what had been an uneasy peace for several years.

The Army recruited him for service as a scout during this time. He knew the country and the Indians. He continued with that work until about 1877 when he took his first job in law enforcement. He became a deputy sheriff in Ford County, Kansas, the county in which Dodge City was located.

By 1884 he had tried his hand at more than one thing around Dodge City; he owned a small ranch in the area and had been a part owner of a saloon for a short time. He was well known and well respected by that time. During that year, the mayor asked him to leave his job as deputy sheriff for the county to become the city marshal. When he took office, his friends presented him with one of the fanciest badges ever worn by a lawman. It was made from two twenty-dollar gold pieces. It was engraved on the back with the words, "William Tilghman, from your many friends, Dodge City, 1884."

During the next two years things got a lot quieter in Dodge. Tilghman asked for and then enforced an ordinance against carrying guns in the city. There was some resistance but not as much as had been expected. He won a lot of support when the people found that he would enforce the law impartially. At least once, when he was challenged on the subject of carrying guns, there was a surprising result.

When two toughs rode into town and announced their intention of taking the marshal down a notch or two, he went looking for them. He found them in a saloon and told them they would have to give up their weapons. When they refused and it looked like they were intending to both draw on the marshal, the crowd in the saloon jumped them and took the guns away from them and handed them over to Bill.

It didn't last long. It was only a couple of years before the railroads were extended and railheads were created closer to the sources of the Texas cattle that supported the economy of Dodge City. Business began to dry up, and the great blizzard of 1886 destroyed the beginnings of a ranching industry in Kansas and points north and west.

Bill tried to hang on for a while, but when land was opened to homesteading in the "unassigned lands" of Indian Territory in 1889 he made the Run and claimed a city lot in Guthrie. He was one of about ten thousand inhabitants who arrived by nightfall of that first day. He was the one whose name came up when the leaders of the new town needed someone to enforce some peace and order. He and his deputy, Jim Masterson, the brother of the famous Bat Masterson, cleared the streets of tents and belongings of people who mistakenly or illegally tried to establish themselves in the marked public thoroughfares.

He built a commercial building for rent on his lot and started saving money to get back into ranching. Before long he had a nice place on Bell Cow Creek near Chandler and had moved his family into a big log cabin. They were settled again. Bill planted a peach orchard, raised corn and alfalfa, and, his main love, bred horses for sale and to race. It was only a short time before the law would call again. The newly appointed United States marshal for the Oklahoma Territory E. D. Nix wanted to talk to Tilghman.

Nix asked for advice. He had announced that he would not hire gunfighters or anyone who drank for the position of deputy marshal. He took a lot of teasing for that. When he asked Bill if he were looking for the wrong kind of men, Tilghman told him that the general idea was right. Bill's concept of the right kind of law enforcement officer was one who was very good with his weapons and confident in his ability but who was loathe to use them. The conversation ended with Nix swearing in a new deputy, William Tilghman.

Nix sent Bill to help clean up the town of Perry along with Heck Thomas, and that started his reputation in the Territory that led to his being called one of The Three Guardsmen of Oklahoma. He served the federal court as a deputy marshal for several years.

Not all of Bill's battles were with bad men. He and Chris Madsen had been on the trail of the Doolin gang awhile but never managed to be in the right place at the right time. They finally figured out that every time the Doolins struck somewhere, they had a report of someone seeing two young women in the area. They were known as Cattle Annie and Little Britches. In or near their teens, they liked to dress like cowboys and had been traveling heavily armed. When Bill realized they were probably acting as lookouts for the Doolins, he took Deputy Steve Burke and went out to arrest them. They could at least make things harder on the outlaws.

They arrived at the farmhouse where the two were staying, but they were spotted. Little Britches ran out, jumped on a horse, and headed out at a hard run. Bill told Burke to get Cattle Annie, and he went after the runaway.

As he started to catch up, Little Britches started throwing shots at him back over her shoulder. He could hardly see shooting a seventeen-year-old girl, but he had to do something. He pulled up and took careful aim with his Winchester and killed her horse.

When her mount went down the girl lost her gun, and before she could get it back, Bill was there. The next few minutes were about as desperate a fight as Tilghman ever survived. He was clawed and kicked and bit but finally got the girl outlaw under control and headed back for the house.

When he got there, Burke was in about the same condition. Annie had jumped out of a window onto his back and the battle was on. The law won, and the two young ladies were arrested. Tilghman knew he could not prove that they were helping the Doolins, but he could prove that they had stolen horses. They each got ten years at Farmington Reform School in Massachusetts.

After his wife, Flora, died of consumption, Bill set up a stud farm near Chandler. He was famous now for his part in ending the raiding of the Doolins, and business was good. It didn't matter; he couldn't stay away from law enforcement. He went on to be sheriff of Lincoln County for two terms then decided to concentrate on horse raising. Again, it was short-lived. He went to Mexico to find and arrest a criminal at the special request of Teddy Roosevelt.

His reputation spread even more, and soon he was asked to become the chief of police for Oklahoma City. He took two years to reorganize and train the force, then returned to the farm. The next call was a little different.

He was soon involved directing the movie *The Passing of the Oklahoma Outlaws*, with help from Chris Madsen and financial backing furnished by E. D. Nix. It was their answer to the one made by Al Jennings, called *Beating Back*. Jenning's film did not show the law enforcement personnel of the time in a good light.

Bill Tilghman met his end in the little oil boomtown of Cromwell, Oklahoma, in 1924. He had been talked into coming out of retirement once more, at age seventy, to try to settle the town as he had done so many times before. He died when he tried to arrest a drunken federal prohibition agent on the street. He had disarmed the man, but before he could check for another weapon the man, Wiley Lynn, pulled a small hideout pistol and shot the old lawman to death.

No question about it, this was the end of one of the best of the "good guys."

Bill Tilghman
(photo courtesy of the University of Oklahoma Libraries)

A Note Concerning Diversity

I started this project with certain expectations, both conscious and, as it turned out, unconscious. I had long felt that some of the best of the old-time lawmen had been ignored, at least in the popular depictions of the West. I wanted to expose the careers of men like Jeff Milton, John Slaughter, Chris Madsen, and Bill Tilghman to a wider audience. I was sure that there would be others when I started looking. I thought I knew the characteristics that I would find in those men. I was sure that they would be like the men with whose careers I was already familiar. They would have similar origins—be of white, mostly Anglo-Saxon ancestry.

Then I discovered the legacy of black lawmen Bass Reeves and Grant Johnson. I became interested in the question of just who these men were whose lives and careers created the idea of the western lawman, the man in the white hat. They obviously were more of a cross section of the population of the West than I had realized. That was my shortsightedness. I knew the truth that the people who built the West came from many different histories and cultures. I never thought to apply that to the question of who it was who brought law and order to the difficult times and places of the frontier.

As intriguing as I hope you will find the stories in this book, I found the bits and pieces of many more as I looked. There are the stories of men who served in the "lighthorse" police of the various Indian Nations; Burton Mossman and the men who served under him in the Arizona Rangers; men like Cesario Lucero, John Swain, and "Old Bat" who worked for and aided John Slaughter. There were "good guys," both black and white, who served in the much reviled Texas State Police during that reconstruction organization's short existence.

Even more to my surprise I discovered that some of the "good guys" may not even have been "guys." There are a couple of newspaper articles from the 1890s which mention three women in two different federal jurisdictions who were commissioned as U.S. deputy marshals for field duty. The papers specifically point out how unusual it was for women to work in the field, carry weapons, and serve warrants. In one case, the prompting for the article was the arrival of one of these deputies with a load of prisoners gathered up in the Indian Territory. She and another officer had brought them in to face the federal court at Paris, Texas.

The point is simply this, the movies and stories we grew up with short changed us just as they short changed the memories of many of these "good guys." It happened because some of these men did not fit a stereotype created by prejudice, bad memory, and the devices of fiction.

Bibliography

Books

Burton, Art. *Black, Red, and Deadly.* (Austin, TX: Eakin Publications, Inc., 1991)

Collier, William Ross and Edwin Victor Westrate. *Hands Up: or Twenty Years of Detective Life in the Mountains and on the Plains.* (Norman, OK: University of Oklahoma Press, 1958)

Croy, Homer. *Trigger Marshal: The Story of Chris Madsen.* (New York City, NY: Duell, Sloan and Pearce, 1958)

Erwin, Allen A. *The Southwest of John H. Slaughter.* (Glendale, CA: Arthur H. Clark Company, 1965)

Haley, J. Evetts. *Jeff Milton: Good Man With a Gun.* (Norman, OK: University of Oklahoma Press, 1948)

James, Marquis. *The Cherokee Strip.* (Norman, OK: University of Oklahoma Press, 1993)

Metz, Leon Claire. *The Shooters.* (New York City, NY: The Berkley Publishing Company, 1976)

Miller, Floyd. *Bill Tilghman: Marshal of the Last Frontier.* (Garden City, NY: Doubleday & Company, Inc., 1968)

Nix, Evertt Dumas. *Oklahombres: Particularly the Wilder Ones.* as told to Gordon Hines (St. Louis, MO: Eden Press, 1929)

O'Neal, Bill. *Encyclopedia of Western Gun-Fighters.* (Norman, OK: University of Oklahoma Press, 1979)

Schaefer, Jack. *Heroes Without Glory.* (New York City, NY: Primus Donald J. Fine, Inc., 1965)

Bibliography

Shirley, Glenn. *The Fourth Guardsman: James Franklin "Bud" Ledbetter.* (Austin, TX: Eakin Press, 1997)

_____. *Heck Thomas: Frontier Marshal. The Story of a Real Gunfighter.* (Philadelphia, PA: Chilton Company, 1962)

_____. *Law West of Fort Smith: Frontier Justice in the Indian Territory, 1834-1896.* (New York City, NY: Collier Books, 1957)

_____. *Temple Houston: Lawyer With a Gun.* (Norman, OK: University of Oklahoma Press, 1980)

Stahlman Speer, Bonnie. *Portrait of a Lawman.* (Norman, OK: Reliance Press, 1996)

Sterling, W. W. *Trails and Trials of a Texas Ranger.* (Norman, OK: University of Oklahoma Press, 1959)

White, Dale. *Fast-Draw Tilghman.* (New York City, NY: Julian Messner, Inc., 1959)

Index

Index

Index